MINDFULNESS
for
BEGINNERS

ALSO BY JON KABAT-ZINN

Books

Mindfulness: Diverse Perspectives on its Meaning, Origins, and Applications
(editor, with J. Mark G. Williams)

The Mind's Own Physician (editor, with Richard J. Davidson)

Letting Everything Become Your Teacher

Arriving at Your Own Door

The Mindful Way Through Depression
(with Mark Williams, John Teasdale, and Zindel Segal)

Coming to Our Senses

Everyday Blessings (with Myla Kabat-Zinn)

Wherever You Go, There You Are

Full Catastrophe Living

Audios from Sounds True

Mindfulness Meditation for Pain Relief

The Mindful Way Through Depression
(with Mark Williams, John Teasdale, and Zindel Segal)

Mindfulness for Beginners

Guided Mindfulness Meditation — Series 1 and Series 3

Pebbles and Pearls: Meditations with Jon Kabat-Zinn

Meditation for Optimum Health (with Andrew Weil, MD)

Other Audios and DVDs

Guided Mindfulness Meditation Practice CDs with Jon Kabat-Zinn:
Series 1, 2 and 3 (from Stress Reduction CDs: www.mindfulnesscds.com)

Mindfulness Meditation www.Nightingale.com

The World of Relaxation www.BetterListen.com

Mindfulness Meditation in Everyday www.BetterListen.com

Exercises and Meditations www.BetterListen.com

JON KABAT-ZINN

MINDFULNESS
for
BEGINNERS

reclaiming the present moment—

and your life

SOUNDS TRUE
Boulder, Colorado

Sounds True, Inc.
Boulder, CO 80306

Sounds True is a trademark of Sounds True, Inc.

Published 2012, 2016

Cover and book design by Karen Polaski
Cover photo © Olga Lyubkina/Shutterstock

Printed in Canada

ISBN: 978-1-62203-667-7

Kabat-Zinn, Jon.
Mindfulness for beginners : reclaiming the present moment—and your life / Jon Kabat-Zinn
p. cm.
Includes bibliographical references.
ISBN 978-1-60407-658-5 (hardcover)
1. Meditation. 2. Awareness. I. Title.
BF637.M4K227 2012
158.1—dc23
2011035941

eBook ISBN: 978-1-60407-753-7

10 9 8

for the perpetual beginner in each of us

Contents

CONTENTS

Introduction

• • •

Welcome to the practice of mindfulness. You may not know it, but if you are coming to the systematic cultivation of mindfulness for the first time, you may very well be on the threshold of a momentous shift in your life, something subtle and, at the same time, potentially huge and important, which just might change your life. Or, to put it differently, you may discover that cultivating mindfulness has a way of giving your life back to yourself, as many people who get involved with mindfulness practice through mindfulness-based stress reduction tell us it has for them. If mindfulness does wind up changing your life in some profound way, it will not be because of this book, although it could possibly be instrumental, and I hope it will be. But any change that comes about in your life will be primarily because of your own efforts—and perhaps in part because of the mysterious impulses that draw us to things before we really know what they are: intimations of what might be emanating from a deep intuition that we discover is truly trustworthy.

Mindfulness is awareness, cultivated by paying attention in a sustained and particular way: on purpose, in the present moment, and non-judgmentally. It is one of many forms of meditation, if you think of meditation as any way in which we engage in (1) systematically regulating our attention and energy (2) thereby influencing and possibly transforming the quality of our experience (3) in the service of realizing the full range of our humanity and of (4) our relationships to others and the world.

1

Ultimately, I see mindfulness as a love affair — with life, with reality and imagination, with the beauty of your own being, with your heart and body and mind, and with the world. If that sounds like a lot to take in, it is. And that is why it can be so valuable to experiment systematically with cultivating mindfulness in your life, and why your intuition to enter into this way of being in relationship to your experience is so healthy.

In the spirit of full disclosure, this book started off as a Sounds True audio program — one that people found useful over the years. One CD included guided meditation practices, and these are the guided meditations that you will find accompanying this book and described in Part 5. As you will come to learn, if you don't know it already, the transformative potential of meditation in general and mindfulness in particular lies in engaging in ongoing practice.

There are two complementary ways to do this: formally and informally. Formally means engaging in making some time every day to practice — in this case with the guided meditations. Informally means letting the practice spill over into every aspect of your waking life in an uncontrived and natural way. These two modes of embodied practice go hand in hand and support each other, and ultimately become one seamless whole, which we could call living with awareness or wakefulness. My hope is that you will make use of the guided meditations on a regular basis as a launching platform for an ongoing exploration of both formal and informal mindfulness practice, and see what happens over the ensuing days, weeks, months, and years.

As we shall see, the very intention to practice with consistency and gentleness — whether you feel like it or not on any given day — is a powerful and healing discipline. Without such motivation, especially at the beginning, it is difficult for mindfulness to take root and go beyond being a mere concept or script, no matter how attractive it might be to you philosophically.

The first CD in the original audio program described the practice of mindfulness and explained why it might be valuable to engage in its cultivation to begin with. That material nucleated the text of this book, which now goes far beyond the original program and content in terms of scope, detail, and depth. Still, I have kept more or less to the original order of topics. I have also kept the voicing mostly in the first- and second-person singular and the first-person plural, on purpose, in the hope that it will maintain the quality of a conversation and mutual inquiry.

In both the text and in the audio program, we will be exploring together the subject of mindfulness as if you'd never heard about it and had no idea what it is or, for that matter, why it might be worth integrating into your life. Primarily, we will be exploring the heart of mindfulness practice and how to cultivate it in your everyday life. We will also touch briefly on what its various health benefits might be in terms of dealing with stress, pain, and illness, and on how people with medical conditions make use of mindfulness practices in the context of mindfulness-based stress reduction (MBSR) programs. We will point out new and exciting areas of scientific research showing that mindfulness training in the form of MBSR actually seems to change both the structure and the functioning of the brain in interesting and important ways, and what some of the implications of this might be for how we relate to our thoughts and our emotions, especially our most reactive ones.

Of necessity, we will only touch on many of these topics. Their elaboration and flowering is an ongoing adventure — and the work of a lifetime. You can think of this volume as the front door to a magnificent edifice, like, say, the Louvre. Only the edifice is yourself and your life and your potential as a human being. The invitation is to enter and then explore, in your own way and at your own pace, the richness and depth of what is available to you — in this case, awareness in all its concrete and specific manifestations.

My hope is that this book will provide you with an adequate conceptual framework for understanding why it makes sense to engage wholeheartedly and on a regular basis in something that seems so much like nothing. While mindfulness and the current high levels of public and scientific interest in it may indeed appear to some to be much ado about nothing, I think it is much more accurate to describe it as *much ado about what might seem like almost nothing that turns out to be just about everything.* We are going to experience firsthand that "almost nothing." It contains a whole universe of life-enhancing possibilities.

Mindfulness as a practice provides endless opportunities to cultivate greater intimacy with your own mind and to tap into and develop your deep interior resources for learning, growing, healing, and potentially for transforming your understanding of who you are and how you might live more wisely and with greater well-being, meaning, and happiness in this world.

Once you establish a robust platform of practice using this book and its guided meditations, there are practically endless resources available if you want to explore mindfulness further. Connecting with the writings of superb teachers, past and present, can be invaluable at one point or another as your mindfulness practice matures and deepens. And if you make the effort to go on retreat with some of the great teachers of today, that could also be an essential catalyst in strengthening and deepening your practice. I highly recommend it.

Much of what I will be saying here is mapped out in much greater detail in other books that I have written, in particular *Full Catastrophe Living; Wherever You Go, There You Are;* and *Coming to Our Senses. Mindfulness for Beginners* is meant to provide a straightforward, convenient portal into the essentials of mindfulness practice, including its formal cultivation and the essence of applying it in everyday life. Both will wind up being part of your ongoing work if you decide to say "yes" to the invitation.

The chapters here are by design brief rather than comprehensive. They are meant to stimulate reflection and encourage you to practice. Over time, as your practice takes root and deepens, as it will if you keep at it, these words may take on different meanings for you. Just as no two moments are the same

4

and no two breaths are the same, each time you reflect on a chapter and bring what it is pointing to into the laboratory of your meditation practice and your life, it is likely to strike you differently. As you will come to know through your direct experience, there is a certain trajectory of deepening in the practice that will carry you along like a river. As you are carried along by the momentum of practice, you may discover, over time, an interesting conjunction between your own experience and what the words here are pointing to.

In launching yourself into the practice, you might want to experiment with choosing a particular guided meditation and playing with it for a few days to see how it feels and what it evokes in you. It is not just a matter of listening to it. The invitation is to participate, to give yourself over to the practice wholeheartedly moment by moment by moment as best you can. You can then use the text to round out the experience by investigating and questioning your understanding of what you are actually asking of yourself as you make the effort to pay close attention to aspects of life we so often ignore entirely or discount as trivial and unimportant.

In a very real sense, you are embarking on what I hope will be an ongoing adventure of inquiry and discovery about the nature of your mind and heart and how you might live with greater presence, openheartedness, and authenticity — not merely for yourself, but for your interconnected embeddedness with those you love, with all beings, and with the world itself. The world in all its aspects may be the greatest beneficiary of your care and attention in this regard.

Deep listening is the essence of mindfulness — a cultivating of intimacy with your own life unfolding, as if it really mattered. And it does. More than you think. And more than you can possibly think.

So, as you embark on this adventure in living, may your mindfulness practice grow and flower and nourish your life and work from moment to moment and from day to day.

PART I

ENTERING

Beginner's Mind

It tends to be a momentous occasion to intentionally stop all your outward activity and, just as an experiment, sit or lie down and open to an interior stillness with no other agenda than to be present for the unfolding of your moments — perhaps for the first time in your adult life.

● ● ●

The people I know who have incorporated the practice of mindfulness into their lives remember quite vividly what drew them to it in the first place, including the feeling tone and life circumstances that led up to that moment of beginning. I certainly do. The emotional topology of the moment of beginning — or even of the moment of realizing that you want to connect with yourself in such a way — is rich and unique for each of us.

Suzuki Roshi, the Japanese Zen Master who founded the San Francisco Zen Center and touched the hearts of so many, is famous for having said, "In the beginner's mind, there are many possibilities, but in the expert's there are few." Beginners come to new experiences not knowing so much and therefore open. This openness is very creative. It is an innate characteristic of the mind. The trick is never to lose it. That would require that you stay in the ever-emerging wonder of the present moment, which is always fresh. Of course you will lose beginner's mind in one way, when you cease to be a beginner. But if you can remember from time to time that each moment is fresh and new, maybe, just maybe, what you know will not get in the way of being open to what you don't know, which is always a larger field. Then a beginner's mind will be available in any moment you are open to it.

The Breath

Take the breath, for instance.
We take it so much for granted. Unless, that is, you have a
bad cold or can't breathe easily for some reason or another.
Then all of a sudden, the breath may become
the only thing in the world you are interested in.

• • •

Yet the breath is coming in and going out of your body all the time. The fact
is that we are being breathed. We drink in the air on each in-breath, giving it back to the world on each out-breath. Our lives depend on it. Suzuki
Roshi referred to its coming in and going out over and over again as "a swinging door." And since we can't leave home without this vital and mysterious
"swinging door," our breathing can serve as a convenient first object of attention to bring us back into the present moment, because we are only breathing
now — the last breath is gone, the next one hasn't come yet — it is always a
matter of this one. So it is an ideal anchor for our wayward attention. It keeps
us in the present moment.

This is one of many reasons why paying attention to the sensations of
breathing in the body serves as the first object of attention for beginning students in many different meditative traditions. But attending to the feeling of
the breath in the body is not only a beginner's practice. It may be simple,
but the Buddha himself taught that the breath has within it everything you

11

would ever need for cultivating the full range of your humanity, especially your capacity for wisdom and for compassion.

The reason, as we shall see shortly, is that paying attention to the breath is not primarily about the breath, nor is paying attention to any other object that we might choose as an object of attention primarily about that object. Objects of attention help us to attend with greater stability. Gradually we can come to feel what the attending itself is all about. It is about the relationship between what seems like the perceiver (you) and the perceived (whatever object you are attending to). These come together into one seamless, dynamical whole in awareness, because they were never fundamentally separate in the first place.

It is the awareness that is primary.

Who Is Breathing?

I t is a conceit to think that *you* are breathing, even though we say it all the time: "I am breathing."

• • •

Of course you are breathing.

But let's face it. If it were really up to you to keep the breath going, you would have died long ago. You would have gotten distracted by this or that, sooner or later . . . and, whoops, dead. So in a sense, "you," whoever you are, are not allowed anywhere near whatever it is that is responsible for your body breathing. The brain stem takes care of that very nicely. Same for the heartbeat and many other core aspects of our biology. We might have some influence on their expression, especially the breath, but it is not fair to say that we are really doing the breathing. It is far more mysterious and wondrous than that.

As you shall see, this brings into question just who *is* breathing, who is beginning to meditate and cultivate mindfulness, who is even reading these words? We shall be visiting these fundamental questions with a beginner's mind in order to understand what is really involved in the cultivation of mindfulness.

The Hardest Work in the World

I t is only fair for me to point out right from the start, again in the spirit of full disclosure, that the cultivation of mindfulness may just be the hardest work in the world.

• • •

Ironically, to grow into the fullness of who we actually already are is the challenge of a lifetime for each of us as human beings. No one can take on that work for us. It can only be our own undertaking in response to our own calling — and only if we care deeply about living the life that is authentically ours to live, in the face of everything that we may be called to engage with, being human.

At the same time, the *work* of cultivating mindfulness is also *play*. It is far too serious to take too seriously — and I say this in all seriousness! — if for no other reason than because it really is about our entire life. It makes sense for a lightness of being and playfulness to be key elements of the practice of mindfulness, because they are key elements of well-being.

Ultimately, mindfulness can become an effortless, seamless element of our life, a way for our very being to express itself authentically, with integrity. In this regard, no one's trajectory in cultivating mindfulness and the benefits that may come from it is the same as anyone else's. The challenge for each of us is to find out who *we* are and to live our way into our own calling. We do this by paying close attention to all aspects of life as they unfold in the present moment. Obviously, no one else can undertake this work for you, just as no one can live your life for you — no one, that is, except you yourself.

What I have said so far may not make full sense to you. In fact, it can't possibly make complete sense until you take your own seat and extend that gesture over time — until you commit to engaging in the formal and informal cultivation of mindfulness, supported by the aspiration to look and to see for yourself how things might actually be behind the veil of appearances and the stories we are so skilled at telling ourselves about how things are — even though they may not be true at all, or are only partially true.

Taking Care of This Moment

W hen it comes to mindfulness, each of us brings our own genius to adventures of this kind. Moreover, we cannot help but make use of and build on everything that has come before in our lives, even if much of it was — and perhaps still is — painful.

• • •

When it comes right down to it, our entire past, whatever it has been, however much pain and suffering it has included, becomes the very platform for doing the work of inhabiting the present moment with awareness, equanimity, clarity, and caring. You need the past that you have; it is raw clay on the potter's wheel. It is both the work and the adventure of a lifetime not to be trapped in either our past or our ideas and concepts, but rather to reclaim the only moment we ever really have, which is always this one. Taking care of this moment can have a remarkable effect on the next one and therefore on the future — yours and the world's. If you can be mindful in this moment, it is possible for the next moment to be hugely and creatively different — because you are aware and not imposing anything on it in advance.

Mindfulness Is Awareness

As I suggested in the Introduction, my operational definition of mindfulness is that it is *paying attention on purpose in the present moment and non-judgmentally.*

• • •

Sometimes I like to add the phrase "as if your life depended on it," because it does to such a profound extent.

But technically speaking, mindfulness is *what arises when* you pay attention, on purpose, in the present moment, non-judgmentally, and as if your life depended on it. And what arises is nothing other than awareness itself.

Awareness is a capacity that we are all intimately familiar with and yet are simultaneously complete strangers to. So the training in mindfulness that we will be exploring together is really the cultivation of a resource that is already ours. It doesn't require going anywhere, it doesn't require getting anything, but it does require learning how to inhabit another domain of mind that we are, as a rule, fairly out of touch with. And that is what you might call the *being mode* of mind.

Doing Mode and Being Mode

Most of our lives we are absorbed in doing: in getting things done, in going rapidly from one thing to the next, or in multitasking — attempting to juggle a bunch of different things at the very same time.

• • •

Often our lives become so driven that we are moving through our moments to get to better ones at some later point. We live to check things off our to-do list, then fall into bed exhausted at the end of the day, only to jump up the next morning to get on the treadmill once again. This way of living, if you can call it living, is compounded by all the ways in which our lives are now driven by the ever-quickening expectations we place on ourselves and that others place on us and we on them, generated in large measure by our increasing dependence on ubiquitous digital technology and its ever-accelerating effects on our pace of life.

If we are not careful, it is all too easy to fall into becoming more of a *human doing* than a *human being*, and forget *who* is doing all the doing, and why.

This is where mindfulness comes in. Mindfulness reminds us that it is possible to shift from a *doing mode* to a *being mode* through the application of attention and awareness. Then our doing can come out of our being and be much more integrated and effective. What is more, we cease exhausting ourselves so much as we learn to inhabit our own body and the only moment in which we are ever alive — this one.

A Grounding in Science

Just to let you know if you don't already, mindfulness and its applications in health and disease have been a subject of increasing study and discovery over the past thirty-plus years, since the founding of the Stress Reduction Clinic and MBSR in 1979 at the University of Massachusetts Medical Center.

• • •

Mindfulness training in the form of MBSR and related interventions has been shown to be highly effective in reducing stress and stress-related medical problems as well as anxiety, panic, and depression in medical patients; in helping them learn to live more effectively and fully with chronic pain conditions; in enhancing quality of life for cancer patients and people with multiple sclerosis; and in reducing relapse in people with a history of major depressive disorder who are at very high risk for relapse. These are just a few of the many clinical findings reported in the scientific literature. MBSR has also been shown to positively affect the way the brain processes difficult emotions under stress, shifting activation in particular areas of the prefrontal cortex from right-sided activation to left-sided activation — in the direction of greater emotional balance — and to induce positive immune system changes that correlate with the brain changes.

Other studies have discovered that people trained in MBSR show activation in networks in the cerebral cortex that are involved in the direct experiencing of the present moment. People not trained in MBSR show less activation in such circuits and greater activation in networks that involve generating narratives *about* one's experiences. These findings suggest that mindfulness practice develops a broader repertoire of ways of experiencing oneself and influences the degree to which we build stories about our experiences that may eclipse or color the experiences themselves.

It is now becoming apparent that MBSR training also results in structural changes in the brain in the form of thickening of certain brain regions, such as the hippocampus, which plays important roles in learning and memory, and thinning in other regions, for instance, the right amygdala, a structure in the limbic system that regulates our fear-based reactions such as to perceived threats of one kind or another, including the thwarting of our desires.

There are many other exciting findings in mindfulness research, and more are being reported in the scientific literature every day.

Mindfulness Is Universal

Mindfulness is often described as the heart of Buddhist meditation. Nevertheless, cultivating mindfulness is not a Buddhist activity.

• • •

In essence, mindfulness is universal because it is all about attention and awareness, and attention and awareness are human capacities that are innate in all of us. Still, it is fair to say that, historically speaking, the most refined and developed articulations of mindfulness and how to cultivate it stem from the Buddhist tradition, and Buddhist texts and teachings constitute an invaluable resource for deepening our understanding and appreciation of mindfulness and the subtleties of its cultivation. That is why from time to time, as you've seen, I mention various Buddhist teachers and viewpoints, nuanced via the ways in which the various traditions within Buddhism — such as Chan, Zen, Tibetan, and Theravada — have refined different modes of speaking about the deployment of attention and awareness, in addition to having developed a vast range of different meditative practices, which ultimately can be thought of as different doors into more or less the same room.

That said, it is important for us to keep in mind that the Buddha himself was not a Buddhist and that even the term "Buddhism" was coined by eighteenth-century European scholars, mostly Jesuits, who had little understanding of what the statues of a man sitting in a cross-legged posture on temple altars across Asia were really about.

Wakefulness

Many people are not aware of this, but strictly speaking, the statues we see of the Buddha, as well as other Buddhist art objects, serve as representations of states of mind rather than of a divinity.

• • •

The Buddha himself symbolizes the embodiment of wakefulness. The very title, "the Buddha," means, in Pali — the language in which his teachings were first written down — *the one who has awakened.*

Awakened to what? To the nature of reality and to the potential for freeing oneself from suffering by engaging in a systematic and very practical approach to living.

The Buddha's insights were hard won, coming out of many years devoted to different forms of arduous meditation practices. And as we've just seen, they are also universal, just as all great scientific insights such as the laws of thermodynamics and the law of gravity are universal. The Buddha clearly stated that his experience and his insights apply to any human being and to any human mind, not just to Buddhists or people practicing Buddhist meditation. If they were not universal, they would be of very limited value. Now it is possible to test some of those assertions scientifically.

According to Buddhist scholar Alan Wallace, the Buddha might best be thought of as a genius of a scientist who, given the time in which he lived, had no instruments at his disposal other than his own body and his own mind. He used what he had to great advantage to explore the deep questions that he was interested in, like what is the nature of the mind, what is the nature of suffering, and is it possible to live a life free of bondage and suffering?

Stabilizing and Calibrating
Your Instrument

O f course, as with any
instrument — whether it is a radio telescope, a spectrophotometer,
or a bathroom scale — you have to first calibrate it and stabilize the
platform on which it sits so that you can get reliable readings.

• • •

Some of the meditation practices that the Buddha taught serve to stabilize
and calibrate the mind so that it can do the deep work of seeing into the
actuality of what is being observed. Obviously, if you are trying to look at the
moon but you set up your telescope on a waterbed, it would be hopeless even
to find the moon, never mind keep it in view and study it carefully. Every time
you shifted your posture even a little bit, you would lose the moon completely.

We face a similar situation with our own mind. If we are going to use
the mind to observe and befriend and ultimately understand itself, first we
will have to learn at least the rudiments of how to stabilize it enough so that
it can actually do the work of paying attention in a sustained and reliable
way and thus, of becoming aware of what's going on beneath the surface of
its own activities.

Even our best efforts can easily be thwarted by all the ways in which we
distract ourselves. Our attention is not very stable and is invariably carried
off someplace else a good deal of the time, as you will experience for yourself
with the guided meditations. With ongoing practice, we at least become far

more familiar with the mind's comings and goings; over time, in important ways, the mind learns how to stabilize itself, at least to a degree.

Even a tiny bit of stability, coupled with awareness, is hugely important and transforming, so it is very important not to build some kind of ideal about your mind not wavering or being absolutely stable in order for you to be "doing it right." That may happen in rare moments under particular circumstances, but for the most part, as we will see, it is in the nature of the mind to wave. Knowing that makes a huge difference in how we will approach the meditation practice.

Inhabiting Awareness Is the Essence of Practice

The challenge of mindfulness is to be present for your experience *as it is* rather than immediately jumping in to change it or try to force it to be different.

• • •

Whatever the quality of your experience in a particular moment, what is most important is your awareness of it. Can you make room for awareness of what is unfolding, whether you like what is happening or not, whether it is pleasant or not? Can you rest in this awareness, even for one breath, or even one in-breath, before reacting to try to escape or make things different? Inhabiting awareness is the essence of mindfulness practice, no matter what you are experiencing, whether it arises in formal meditation or in going about your life. Life itself becomes the meditation practice as we learn to take up residency in awareness — this essential dimension of our being that is already ours but with which we are so unfamiliar that we frequently cannot put it to use at the very times in our lives when we need it the most.

But if, through bringing an ongoing intentionality and gentle discipline to both formal and informal practice, mindfulness were to function increasingly as our "default setting" so to speak, our baseline condition that we come back to instinctively when we lose our emotional balance momentarily, then it could serve as a profoundly healthy and reliable resource for us in challenging times. More on this later.

The Beauty of Discipline

As you've no doubt noticed, I used the word *discipline* in speaking about the cultivation of mindfulness . . . and for good reason.

• • •

To cultivate mindfulness really does involve and call out of us a certain constancy of motivation and purpose in the face of all sorts of energies in our lives, some from inside ourselves and some from outside, that dissipate our awareness by perpetually distracting us and diverting us from our intentions and purpose. The discipline I am referring to is really the willingness to bring the spaciousness and clarity of awareness back over and over again to whatever is going on — even as we feel we are being pulled in a thousand different directions.

Just taking this kind of stance toward our own experience, without trying to fix or change anything at all, is an act of generosity toward oneself, an act of intelligence, an act of kindness.

The word *discipline* comes from *disciple,* someone who is in a position to learn. So when we bring a certain discipline to the cultivation of mindfulness and are aware of how challenging it is to bring a sustained attending to any aspect of our lives, we are actually creating the conditions for learning something fundamental from life itself. Then life becomes the meditation practice and the meditation teacher, and whatever happens in any moment is simply *the curriculum* of that moment.

The real challenge is how will we be in relationship to whatever is arising? Here is where freedom itself is to be found. Here is where a moment of genuine happiness might be experienced, a moment of equanimity, a moment of peace. Each moment is an opportunity to see that we do not have to succumb to old habits that function below the level of our awareness. With great intentionality and resolve, we can experiment with non-distraction. We can experiment with non-diversion. We can experiment with non-fixing. We can experiment with non-doing.

If we are willing to encounter our old habits in this way, without turning non-distraction and non-doing into unattainable ideals, and if we can bring gentleness and kindness to the process over and over again for even the briefest of moments, then we might taste the very real possibility of being at home and at peace with things exactly as they are without having to try to change or fix anything in this moment.

When it comes right down to it, this orientation constitutes not only a gentle and healing discipline. It is a radical act of love . . . and of sanity.

Adjusting Your Default Setting

What is unfolding
when nothing much of anything is going on with you?

● ● ●

I encourage you to check out for yourself what is going on at such times. For most of us, usually it is thinking. Thinking is going on. It takes lots of different forms.

Thinking seems to constitute our "default setting" rather than awareness.

It is a good thing to notice, because in this way, we might slowly shift from this automatic reverting to thinking over and over again to another mode of mind that may stand us in far better stead, namely awareness itself. Perhaps over time we can adjust our default setting to one of greater mindfulness rather than of mindlessness and being lost in thought.

As soon as you take your seat or lie down to meditate, the first thing you will notice is that the mind has a life of its own. It just goes on and on and on: thinking, musing, fantasizing, planning, anticipating, worrying, liking, disliking, remembering, forgetting, evaluating, reacting, telling itself stories — a seemingly endless stream of activity that you may not have ever noticed in quite this way until you put out the welcome mat for a few moments of non-doing, of just being.

And what is more, now that you have decided to cultivate greater mindfulness in your life, your mind is at risk for filling up with a host of new ideas and opinions — about meditation, about mindfulness, about how well you're doing or not doing, about whether you are doing it right — in addition to all the other ideas and opinions swirling around in the mind.

It is a bit like television sports commentary. There is what is actually going on in the game, and then there is the endless commentary. When you begin a formal meditation practice, it is almost inevitable that you will now be subject to meditation commentary to one degree or another. It can fill the space of the mind. Yet it is not the meditation any more than the play-by-play is the game itself.

Sometimes shutting off the sound on the television can allow you to actually watch the game and take it in in an entirely different and more direct way — a first-order, first-person experience — rather than filtered through the mind of another. In the case of meditation it is the same, except your own thoughts are doing the broadcast commentary, turning a first-order direct experience of the moment into a second-order story about it: how hard it is, how great it is, and on and on and on.

On some occasions your thoughts might tell you how boring meditation is, how silly you were for thinking that this non-doing approach might be of any value, given that it seems to bring up a good deal of discomfort, tension, boredom, and impatience. You might find yourself questioning the value of awareness, wondering, for instance, how awareness of how uncomfortable you are could possibly "liberate" you, or reduce your stress and anxiety, or help you in any way at all above and beyond just wasting time and succumbing to endless tedium.

This is what the thought-stream does, and that is precisely why we need to become intimate with our minds through careful observation. Otherwise, thinking completely dominates our lives and colors everything we feel and do and care about. And you are not special in this regard. Everybody has a similar thought-stream running 24/7, often without realizing it at all.

Awareness: Our Only Capacity Robust Enough to Balance Thinking

For the most part, it was never pointed out by our parents or teachers, and no suggestion was made during our educational trajectory, that maybe *awareness of thinking* could provide some kind of balance and perspective so that our thoughts didn't rule our lives, unbeknownst to us.

• • •

Let's reflect for a moment.

Is it not true that ever since we were in school, we were trained to think "properly," to think critically? Isn't that a good deal of what school is for? I remember very clearly asking my teachers at Humboldt Junior High School in New York City, when it came to learning something that I did not like or want to learn, such as trigonometry or grammar, "Why do we have to learn this?" Usually, when the teacher didn't just get angry but took the question seriously, the response was that it would help us develop the capacity to think critically and to speak and reason more clearly and more thoughtfully.

And you know what? It turns out that is true. We certainly do need a foundation in critical thinking and in analytical and deductive reasoning in order to understand the world and not be totally lost or overwhelmed by it. So thinking — precise, keen, critical thinking — is an extremely important faculty we need to develop, refine, and deepen. But it is not the only capacity we have that needs developing, refining, and deepening. There is another equally important faculty that almost never gets any systematic attention or training in school, and that is the faculty of awareness. Yet awareness is at least as important and useful to us as thinking. In fact, it is demonstrably more powerful in that any thought, no matter how profound, can be held in awareness.

Attention and Awareness
Are Trainable Skills

Probably what teachers most want is to have their students' sustained attention.

• • •

But this itself is hard to get unless the teacher is able to make the subject matter of the moment, whatever it is, come alive, to make it compelling and relevant within a classroom atmosphere of safety, inclusion, and belonging, along with a sense of learning as an adventure. It doesn't help to yell at a class to pay attention when the children are being unruly. But it can help a lot — in fact, it can be a precious gift — to teach students the *how* of paying attention themselves and turning the process itself into something of an adventure.

Paying attention is a trainable skill, capable of ongoing refinement. As no less a luminary than William James, the father of American psychology, well knew, attention and the awareness that arises from it are the doorway to true education and learning — life-long gifts that keep deepening with use. It may very well be that the capacity to rest in awareness without distraction, in addition to simply balancing the power of thought and bringing a wiser perspective to it, may give rise to an entirely different *kind* of thinking.

It may be that future research will show that mindfulness training actually enhances creativity, freeing the mind to produce less routinized kinds of thoughts and freer and more imaginative associations.

Nothing Wrong with Thinking

When we speak about
the value of cultivating and refining our capacity for attention and the
awareness that arises from it as ways to balance the thought process,
it is important to stress that there is nothing wrong with thinking.

• • •

Our capacity for thought is one of humanity's most amazing qualities. Just
think of all of the great works of science, mathematics, and philosophy. They
are all examples of the flowering of thought, as are poetry and literature,
music, and all the great works of human culture. All this comes out of the
human mind, and much of it out of our capacity to think.

But when thinking is not held and examined in the larger field of awareness, it can run amuck. Coupled with our unexamined afflictive emotional
states, our thinking can wind up causing great suffering . . . for ourselves, for
others, and sometimes for the world.

Befriending Our Thinking

I t is very important as a beginner that you understand right from the start that meditation is about *befriending* your thinking, about holding it gently in awareness, no matter what is on your mind in a particular moment. It is not about shutting off your thoughts or changing them in any way.

• • •

Meditation is not suggesting that it would be better if you didn't think and were simply to suppress all those sometimes unruly, disturbing, and disquieting, sometimes uplifting and creative thoughts when they arise.

If you do try to suppress your thinking, you are just going to wind up with a gigantic headache. Such a pursuit is unwise, pure folly — like trying to stop the ocean from waving. It is the very nature of the ocean for its surface to change as a result of changing atmospheric conditions. At times, when there are no currents or wind, the surface of the ocean can be mirrorlike, completely flat and calm. But usually, it is waving to one degree or another on the surface. In the midst of a storm, a typhoon or a hurricane, the surface can be ferociously turbulent. It may not even look like a surface any more. Yet even in the midst of the most ferocious turbulence, if you descend beneath the surface thirty or forty feet or so, you will find no turbulence at all . . . just gentle undulation.

The mind is similar. The surface can be extremely labile, changing constantly with the changing "weather patterns" of our lives: our emotions, moods, thoughts, our experiences, everything, often with little or no aware-ness on our part. We can feel victimized by our thoughts, or blinded by them. We can easily mis-take them for the truth or for reality when in actuality they are just waves on its surface, however tumultuous they may be at times.

The entirety of our mind, on the other hand, is by its very nature deep, vast, intrinsically still and quiet, like the depths of the ocean.

Images of Your Mind
That Might Be Useful

The ocean is not the only metaphor for the mind, and waves are not the only metaphor for thoughts. There are many useful images that might provide new angles and novel approaches for working mindfully with thoughts and the process of thinking.

• • •

For instance, thoughts can be likened to the bubbles coming off the bottom of a pot of boiling water: they nucleate at the bottom, rise to the surface, and dissipate unimpeded into the air. Alternatively, you might imagine the energy of the thinking mind as the flowing of water in a stream or a great river. We can either be caught up in the stream and carried away by it, or we can sit on the bank and apprehend its various patterns with our eyes — the eddies and whirlpools ever-arising, changing form, and passing away — and with our ears as we drink in its various gurgles and songs. Sometimes thoughts cascade through the mind like a waterfall. We might take some delight in this image, and visualize ourselves sitting behind the torrent in a little cave or depression in the rock, aware of the ever-changing sounds, astonished by the unending roar, resting in the timelessness of the cascading mind in such an extended moment.

The Tibetans sometimes describe thoughts as *writing on water,* in essence empty, insubstantial, and transient. I love that. Skywriting is another apt image. Touching soap bubbles is another lovely metaphor. In all of these images, thoughts can be seen to "self-liberate," to go *poof* just like soap bubbles when they are touched, or in our case when they are "touched" by awareness itself — in other words, when they are recognized as thoughts, simply events arising, lingering, and passing away in a boundless and timeless field of awareness.

We see that thoughts, when brought into and held in awareness in this way, readily lose their power to dominate and dictate our responses to life, no matter what their content and emotional charge. They then become workable rather than imprisoning. And thus, we become a bit freer in the knowing and the recognizing of them as events in the field of awareness. They become workable without our having to do any work — it is the awareness that does all the work and the liberating.

Not Taking Our Thoughts Personally

Ⅰt is a big step toward reclaiming
our lives when we realize that, no matter what their content, good,
bad, or ugly, we do not have to take our thoughts personally.

• • •

We do not have to believe them. We do not have to even think of them as "ours." We can recognize them simply as thoughts, as *events in the field of awareness,* events that arise and pass away very rapidly, that sometimes carry insights, sometimes enormous emotional charge, and that can have a huge effect for better or for worse in our lives, *depending on how we are in relationship to them.*

When we don't automatically take them personally or believe the stories about "reality" that we build from them, when we can simply hold them in awareness with a sense of curiosity and wonder at their amazing power given their insubstantiality, their limitations, and inaccuracies, then we have a chance right in that moment, in any moment really, to not get caught in their habitual patterning, to see thoughts for what they are, impersonal events, and instead be the knowing that awareness already is.

Then, in that moment at least, we are already free, ready to act with greater clarity and kindness within the constantly changing field of events that is nothing other than life unfolding — not always as we think it should, but definitely as it is.

Selfing

Whatever metaphors or images we find helpful for describing the nature of the mind and of our relationship to our thoughts and emotions in meditation and in everyday life, it is important to recognize that they themselves are also thoughts.

● ● ●

If we fall into the thought-stream and get caught up with various thoughts, especially if we self-identify with them — saying to ourselves: that is "me" or that is "not me" — then we are *really* caught. For this is where the ultimate attachment arises, with the identifying of circumstances or conditions or things with the personal pronouns, namely "I," "me," and "mine." Sometimes we call this habit of self-identification *selfing,* the tendency to put ourselves at the absolute center of the universe.

As we shall see, it can be very helpful to pay attention to how much of the time we are engaged in selfing, and without trying to fix it or change it, simply hold that strong habit of mind in awareness.

Our Love Affair with Personal Pronouns — Especially *I, Me,* and *Mine*

The Buddha taught for forty-five years. He is said to have said that all of his teachings could be encapsulated in one sentence. If that is so, perhaps we might want to remember what it was, even if we don't necessarily understand it at first. Imagine forty-five years of profound teaching distilled into one sentence: "Nothing is to be clung to as 'I,' 'me,' or 'mine.'"

• • •

It might be helpful to reflect on what the Buddha might have meant when he used the verb "to cling." "Nothing is to be clung to as 'I,' 'me,' or 'mine'" does not mean there is no "you." It isn't suggesting that perhaps you will have to hire someone to put on your pants in the morning because there's no "you" to do it. Nor does it mean that you should give away all the money in your bank account because it is not yours and there is no real bank anyway. What it means is that *clinging is optional,* that we can recognize it when it arises and choose not to feed it. It means that the selfing habit is a major part of our default setting, that mode of mind that we revert to constantly when we go unconscious or drone on in the automatic pilot *doing* mode. It means that how we relate to all our moments, all our experiences, is a choice. It means that we can make the choice, moment by moment, to recognize how much we *do* cling to "I," "me," and "mine," how self-oriented and self-preoccupied we can be, and then decide not to cling to them, or more reasonably, to catch ourselves when we do. It is saying that we don't have to automatically and with no awareness fall into the habits of self-identification, self-centeredness, and selfing. What is more, if we are open to looking at ourselves afresh, we can readily see that these thought-habits actually distort reality, create illusions and delusions, and ultimately imprison us.

So when you hear yourself using the words "I," "me," and "mine" a great deal, perhaps it can serve as a signal to quietly reflect on where this is taking you and whether it is serving you well.

Awareness Is a Big Container

We have become so highly conditioned by our patterns of thinking that we don't even recognize thoughts as thoughts anymore.

• • •

Is it not the case that we tend to experience our feelings and our thoughts as facts, as the absolute reality of things, even when we know someplace deep within us that that is not entirely the case? Of course we do, but we don't know what do to with that uncomfortable feeling lurking in the shadows of our awareness. In part because it's a bit scary — sometimes even more than a bit scary.

But, as we have seen, we've had little if any guidance or systematic training in the value of relying on our awareness as something other than and bigger than thought and emotion — even though it is obvious that awareness is a big container and can hold any thought, any emotion, without in the slightest being caught by any of it. We are born with this capacity we call awareness, just as we are born with our amazing capacities for thinking and for feeling and of our eyes for seeing. However, it is sorely underdeveloped.

For instance, when did you ever take even one class on the cultivation of awareness, along with all your training in critical thinking? It's doubtful that you ever did. Amazingly, it has not been part of the curriculum in elementary school or middle school or high school or, for that matter, in what we call "higher" education, at least until recently. However, now the situation is changing rapidly, as mindfulness is being introduced in a range of different ways across the entire educational spectrum and for all ages.

The Objects of Attention Are
Not as Important as the Attending Itself

Since mindfulness is about
the cultivation of moment-to-moment awareness through careful,
systematic, and disciplined attending, it can seem at first as if
what we are paying attention *to* — that is, the various possible
objects of attention — is what is most important.

• • •

These objects of attention can be anything within the realm of our experience: what we are seeing, or hearing, or smelling, or tasting, or touching, or feeling, or knowing in any given moment. That is in part because, from the very beginning of a meditation practice, we do have to focus on *something* to pay attention to, whether it is the feeling of the breath moving in and out of our body, or sounds coming to our ears, or anything else we can perceive or apprehend in the present moment. Later on, we may come to realize that we can focus on awareness itself and become aware of awareness, without choosing any particular object to focus on. We will explore this in the last track of the accompanying CD.

But it is essential that you know right from the beginning that it is not the breath sensations, or sounds, or even our thoughts when we are paying attention to thoughts, that are most important.

What is most important but most easily missed, taken for granted, and not experienced is the awareness that feels and knows directly, without thinking, that breathing is going on in this moment, that hearing is going on in this moment, that thoughts are moving through the sky-like space of the mind at this moment. As we have seen, it is the awareness that is of primary importance, no matter what the objects are that we are paying attention to.

And that awareness is already ours. It is already available, already complete, already capable of holding and knowing (non-conceptually) anything and everything in our experience inwardly and outwardly, no matter how big, how trivial, or how momentous. That is simply the property of awareness. And you already have it! Or perhaps it would be more accurate to say, you already *are* it.

PART II

SUSTAINING

Mindfulness-Based Stress Reduction

Since 1979, my colleagues and I at the University of Massachusetts Medical Center's Stress Reduction Clinic have been offering training in mindfulness in the form of Mindfulness-Based Stress Reduction (MBSR) within mainstream medicine to people facing stress, pain, illness, and disease who find they are not receiving full satisfaction from their health care and medical care. At times, they can easily feel as if they are falling through the cracks of the health-care system — or that they fell through a long time ago. And nowadays, thirty-plus years later, there are not just cracks in the health-care system, there are veritable chasms.

• • •

There are vast public debates about how to pay for health care, but what the "care" itself consists of, or even what constitutes robust health and how it can be maintained and restored, often receives far less scrutiny and even less action.

Under such circumstances, it is only wise to take on a degree of responsibility for one's own health and well-being. In fact, this kind of personal engagement in one's own health is an essential element of the new vision of medicine and health care, a much more participatory model in which the patient plays an important collaborative role in mobilizing his or her interior resources for healing to whatever degree possible.

The idea behind MBSR is to challenge people to see if there is something that they can do for themselves — as a vital complement to whatever their doctors and surgeons and the health-care system as a whole can do for them — to help them move toward greater levels of health and well-being across the lifespan, starting from whatever condition they are in when they decide that it is time to engage in this way.

When I say "health and well-being," I mean them on the deepest and broadest of levels. Ultimately they have to do not just with the body's health or with getting people back to some kind of baseline status of not being ill that we consider "normal," but with a condition of optimal mental, emotional, and physical functioning and well-being that you develop through a systematic and disciplined exploring, in the laboratory of your own life, what the true extent of your being human actually is. This is catalyzed by coming to know with greater intimacy your own mind and body, which are not fundamentally separate, through the systematic cultivation of your intrinsic biological and psychological capacities for well-being and wisdom, including the compassion and goodness that lie within all of us.

A World-Wide Phenomenon

MBSR has now spread to clinics, medical centers, and hospitals across the country and around the world. The guided meditations on the CD are similar in some respects to those my colleagues and I use with our patients in the hospital when they take the MBSR program in the Stress Reduction Clinic.

• • •

That doesn't mean this approach is just for people experiencing disease, chronic pain, or mental distress. Being universal, it is applicable to anybody who is motivated to optimize his or her well-being.

As we've seen, mindfulness meditation is really all about awareness: its quality, its stability, its reliability, and its capacity to free us from our own habits of self-diminishment and of ignoring what is most important in our lives. Mindfulness develops bare attention, discernment, clear seeing, and thus wisdom, where "wisdom" means knowing the actuality of things rather than being caught in our misperceptions and misapprehensions of reality. And those misperceptions and misapprehensions tend to be truly legion for all of us, no matter who we are, because it is so easy to be caught up in our own belief systems, ideas, opinions, and prejudices. They form a kind of veil or a cloud that often prevents us from seeing what is right in front of our faces or from acting in ways that truly reflect what we most care about and value. There may be times when our family members try to get through to us — out of love and out of desperation — to point out how much unnecessary suffering we are generating through what we may be refusing to see, or what we are taking so personally that we may be misconstruing it entirely.

But even in such circumstances, it is uncannily hard for anyone to get through to us. Usually we can't hear it or don't believe it, so caught up are we in the momentum of our own delusion and habits of self-distraction.

An Affectionate Attention

While mindfulness is about cultivating bare attention, discernment, clear seeing, and wisdom, at the same time it is important to bring an *affectionate* quality to the attending — an openness to whatever may arise, along with a degree of kindness and a willingness to extend our intrinsic compassion to embrace even ourselves.

• • •

Again, this is not something that we need to force or strive to acquire. Rather it is a quality of being that we might realize is already part of who we are. All we need to do is keep it in mind from time to time for it to come more into the foreground in any moment.

Mindfulness Brought to All the Senses

When I use the term *clear seeing*, it seems to privilege one particular sense. But "seeing," in the way I am using it here, represents all of our senses, because it is only through our senses that we can be aware of and therefore know anything at all.

• • •

From the meditative perspective — especially in Buddhism — there is a recognition that there are more than five senses. This is also the case from the perspective of neuroscience, as we shall see. Buddhism explicitly includes mind as a sixth sense. And by "mind," Buddhists don't mean thinking. They mean awareness, that capacity of mind that knows non-conceptually.

For example, you *know* where you are right now. You don't have to think about it. Most of the time, at least, you just know where you are, and you know what has come before. In other words, you have a sense of orientation in time. You also have a sense of orientation in space. We don't think about it at all, but there's an awful lot that we take for granted that we actually know in very deep ways. It is that cognizant, non-conceptual knowing faculty — awareness itself — that is being pointed to here when we talk about mind as a sixth sense.

In this way, clear seeing also means clear hearing, clear smelling, clear tasting, clear touching, and clear knowing, which would include knowing what's on your mind, and therefore knowing both what you are thinking and what emotions are visiting, and therefore *feeling what you are feeling, grounded in the body,* whether it be fear or anger or sadness, frustration, irritation, impatience, annoyance, satisfaction, empathy, compassion, happiness, or anything else.

In this way, anything and everything can become our teacher of the moment, reminding us of the possibility of being fully present: the gentle caress of air on our skin, the play of light, the look on someone's face, a passing contraction in the body, a fleeting thought in the mind. Anything. Everything. If it is met in awareness.

Proprioception and Interoception

Science also now recognizes that human beings have more than five senses, that we are endowed with additional sensing capacities that are critical to our lives and well-being.

• • •

One is called *proprioception*. "Proprio" means "self." Proprioception is the sense of knowing and feeling the body's position in space both statically and in motion. Very rarely, proprioception can be lost due to neurological damage. Without this sense, the interior sense of the body is lost. The body simply does not function as it did before. Neurologist Oliver Sacks described the consequences to a woman who had lost her sense of proprioception due to a drug reaction. While she appeared normal, she no longer had any sense of the presence of a body, and she could only move her arm to feed herself if she could see it. All fluidity of movement was gone. Her loss was staggering on multiple levels. Just contemplating that what we most take for granted could be lost can cause us to realize how little we pay attention to this essential sense with which our bodies are endowed and upon which our lives depend without our even knowing it.

In addition to proprioception, there is another not-commonly-known sense called *interoception*. This is the sense of knowing how your body is feeling from the inside. It is not based in thinking about how your body is, but on the direct experiencing of it. It is an internal, embodied *feeling*, a felt sense. Someone asks you how you are feeling and you say "fine." How do you know you are fine? Interoception.

In the meditation practices, a great deal of attention is accorded to a sense of the body as a whole, both in sitting meditation and in moving. We can learn to "inhabit" the body with full awareness and to sustain this embodied "presencing" over time.

The Unity of Awareness

Given all the different senses that are available to us, there is quite a bit that we could be aware of when it comes to our lived experience in any moment.

• • •

This includes our outward experience of the world and our inward experience of being, including the body and all its sense impressions, as well as thoughts and emotions. Since awareness, amazingly enough, can hold all of it — both the inner landscape and the outer landscape of our experience — there is no fundamental separation in experience between inner and outer, between the knower and what's being known, between subject and object, between being and doing. There only seems to be.

And there really does *seem* to be a separation. That seeming separation can be a dominant and unquestioned aspect of our experience. What is more, it can obscure the underlying unity of awareness in which there is, mysteriously, just seeing, hearing, smelling, tasting, touching, feeling, knowing, or you could say, just "awarenessing"— and no permanent, unchanging, centralized "you" who is experiencing all of this. Thus, there is no separation between subject ("the seer") and object ("the seen"), although, again, there certainly seems to be — and in a conventional sense, of course it is "you" who is hearing, seeing, smelling, tasting, and knowing. But who are you?

Can you feel the mysteriousness of this inquiry? And the potential value in it?

We will revisit this question shortly.

The Knowing Is Awareness

Think about it for a moment.
"Just seeing" includes the miracle of being able to see and the in-the-moment non-conceptual knowing that you are seeing. "Just hearing" includes the knowing that you are hearing. The knowing is awareness. It is available before thinking sets in. Yet it can also include any and all thoughts when thinking does come into play around seeing, hearing, or any other aspect of experience.

● ● ●

As you saw in the last chapter, I sometimes use *awareness* as a present participle, as if it were a verb: *awarenessing*. There is a particular flavor to saying it in this way which conveys a tonal feeling that is important for the cultivation of mindfulness. Awareness is no longer merely a noun, a thing or a desirable state to be attained and therefore static. It becomes a verb and thus carries a whole dynamic suggesting a process rather than an end state — a dynamic that is critically important to the whole adventure of looking into who we are as human beings and of making use of our capacity to be aware, to be present, to be mindful, and to live more effectively in a very stressful and sometimes highly disordered, chaotic, dis-eased, and sometimes tragic world, a world that is at the same time beautiful in an infinite number of ways.

That beauty includes the inhabitants of this world, its creatures, including ourselves. Including you.

Life Itself Becomes
the Meditation Practice

An intrinsic irony of this perspective on the centrality and unity of awareness — especially when people come to the medical center for training in MBSR with a medical diagnosis and the accompanying sense that there is something wrong with them that needs to be put right — is that in our way of seeing things, they (and we) are already whole, even when we have some kind of problem or disease. And that is why we say to people that from our perspective, as long as you are breathing there is more right with you than wrong with you, no matter what is wrong.

• • •

For those participating in MBSR, we systematically pour energy in the form of attention and awareness into what is already right with us, just as an experiment, and see what happens. We are not ignoring what is wrong, just letting the rest of the health-care team take care of that aspect of things, while we attend to those other very basic elements of our experience — often taken totally for granted — such as that we have a body in the first place, that we are breathing, that we can sense the world in various ways, that the mind generates thoughts and emotions seemingly endlessly, that we have the capacity for kindness toward ourselves and others, that we can be patient and trusting. When we bring these dimensions of our being into awareness, life itself becomes the meditation practice.

You Already Belong

When you undertake this practice with a group of other human beings very much like yourself, as in MBSR classes at the hospital, it becomes even more powerful because you can be inspired and motivated by other people's strength and tenacity and insights, often manifested in the face of unimaginable life circumstances and difficulties.

• • •

And even if you are by yourself, it turns out you are never by yourself, because this kind of inspiration is everywhere when you start to look around.

Moreover, when you are meditating at home, you can know and take comfort and inspiration from the fact that there are literally millions of other people very much like yourself meditating at that very same moment. You are whole and also part of larger and larger circles of wholeness you may not even know about. You are never alone. And you already belong.

You belong to humanity.

You belong to life.

You belong to this moment, to this breath.

Right Beneath Our Noses

Although we are actually already whole — the root meaning of the words *health, healing,* and *holy* — we are unfortunately also in the habit of fragmenting the world into inner and outer, this and that, subject and object, perceiver and perceived, what we like and what we dislike, what we want and what we don't want. So we don't necessarily feel whole at all.

● ● ●

When we are unconsciously caught up in making distinctions that separate and fragment our experience rather than recognizing its intrinsic wholeness, this orientation exerts a profound grip on our habits of thought, emotion, sensing, and knowing. Those unexamined habits of mind are what keep us stuck and prevent us from apprehending the spaciousness, the clarity, the unity of awareness — even though you could say that along with the breath, mindfulness is right beneath our noses in every moment, all puns intended. Thus, mindfulness is always available to us. It is also easily missed if we are not attending, if we ignore the potential of our own presence, if we are not willing to show up and to stop, to look, to listen. It is that simple.

Awareness is already ours by birth and by virtue of being human. We only need to learn to befriend and inhabit this innate capacity of ours.

Here is where the systematic cultivation of mindfulness comes into the picture.

Mindfulness Is Not Merely a Good Idea

Because mindfulness is so popular at the moment, it is very easy to misconstrue what it really involves: "I get it! I will be more present and less judgmental. Good idea! Why didn't I think of that myself? Clear sailing from here on. No problem! I'll just be more mindful."

• • •

But mindfulness is *a way of being*, one that requires consistent cultivation. It is a discipline all its own that naturally extends into all aspects of life as it is unfolding. It is certainly a good idea to be mindful, but mindfulness is not merely a good idea.

And while it is simple, it is not easy. It is not so easy to maintain mindfulness, even over very short periods of time. We saw earlier that in some ways, you could think of it as the hardest work in the world, and the most important.

So until and unless you implement it and sustain it through ongoing, regular practice, leavened with an appropriate attitude of gentleness and kindness toward yourself, mindfulness can easily remain simply one more thought to fill your head and make you feel inadequate . . . one more concept, one more slogan, one more chore, one more thing to schedule into your already too-busy day.

To Come Back in Touch

The real challenge, as we shall see as we engage in the actual *practice* of mindfulness, is that the practice itself gives us instant access to other dimensions of our life that have been here all along, but with which we have been seriously out of touch.

● ● ●

I am using that sensory metaphor of being "out of touch" intentionally, to acknowledge how astonishingly easy it is to be unaware, to be more on the mindless side rather than mindful, to see without really seeing, or hear without hearing, or eat without tasting. In other words, we can easily zone along on autopilot for most of our lives, meanwhile thinking we know what is happening, we know who we are, we know where we are going. That could be said to be our current default setting: the highly conditioned and tenacious mode of unawareness, of automatic pilot, of mindless doing.

This is why the cultivation of mindfulness is both so necessary . . . and so challenging.

Who Am I?
Questioning Our Own Narrative

An interesting thing happens when we start to question and investigate in an open, curious, and systematic way who we are and where we are going. Do we actually know with any clarity or certainty *who* we are, or are we simply creating a gigantic and usually convincing (up to a point) narrative for ourselves that we live inside of without examining?

• • •

When the story seems to be going well, perhaps we feel happy and have a sense of moving full speed ahead into whatever is next. But if the narrative takes a different turn because conditions change or because, perhaps from early childhood, it has been a story with major elements of sadness, abuse, neglect, or not having been seen, then our internal narrative might be one of being inadequate, unworthy, unloveable, or unintelligent — or in which there's no real hope for us.

What mindfulness can do to help in such circumstances is very simple. It reminds us that this internal narration of ours is entirely based on thought. It is a construct, a fabrication that we have gotten comfortable with. It may be an amazing, convincing, absorbing story a good deal of the time. It may also at turns be horrific or boringly normal. But it is a confabulation all the same.

You Are More Than Any Narrative

Our personal internal narratives, as you may have noticed, lend themselves to being easily reinforced by all sorts of evidence that we can and do martial up from the past to bolster whatever contention we care to feature at any moment within the story: such as that we are not good enough, or why we know better than everybody else, or whatever we may be telling ourselves in any given moment or have been telling ourselves for years.

• • •

Yet all such efforts are simply the spinning out of self-centered, self-preoccupied yarns, woven by our thoughts interacting with our experience, usually completely outside of our awareness.

While they may contain elements of truth, these narratives are not the entire truth of who we are. Who you actually are is far bigger than the narrative you construct about who you are. That is the case for all of us. So either we need a much bigger narrative, or we need to see into the intrinsic empty nature of all narrative: that while it may be true to a degree, it is devoid of any essential, enduring finality or truth. Our lives are simply bigger than thought. One example of this is what you are experiencing directly through your senses in this moment, including the sense of being embodied, before you clothe it in any kind of narrative.

It turns out that a recent scientific study from the University of Toronto has shown that there are different networks in the brain for different kinds of self-referencing of experience. One network, termed the Narrative Focus (NF), is active when we build a story based on our experience. It involves a great deal of thinking, often coupled with rumination and worry. A second network, termed the Experiential Focus (EF), is active when we are grounded in what is being experienced in the present moment, when we are very much in the body and in unfolding sensory experience — without all the evaluation of the narrative network. The study found that people who train in MBSR showed an increase in activity in the EF network and a decrease in the activity in the NF network. This is one example of how training in mindfulness can actually influence how the brain processes experience — in this case, how you experience your life unfolding and what you tell yourself about it.

It is not that the EF is superior to the NF. Both are necessary to live an integrated and balanced life. But when the NF predominates, especially out of unawareness, it can very much limit our understanding of ourselves and of what might be possible. The NF can be thought of as the usual default mode. Indeed, it is sometimes called the *default network*. It has been identified in some studies as the area of the cerebral cortex that is most active when we are "not doing anything." The more we train ourselves in living our experience in the present moment without evaluating or judging it so quickly, the more we allow ourselves to simply rest mindfully in our own somatic experience, the more we are shifting the default setting to that of the EF network and the inhabiting of present moment experience.

When you begin to question the narrative of yourself and inquire as to who is even doing all of this talking inside your own head, you may come to realize that you have no idea! You simply don't know. That realization is in itself an important milestone, one that offers an entirely new and much freer way of being with experience. But early on in this process of awakening to not knowing what you thought you knew, you can still feel fragmented, pulled between competing stories, or weighed down by the enormity of the one that is dominating your life at the moment, which is now compounded by the realization that you are not so sure about what you used to be very sure about. This could actually be a very good sign.

You Are Never Not Whole

Within any turmoil and
fragmentation that we may be feeling when we begin to
examine our lives and our minds with greater clarity and
inquisitiveness, we may also find a long-ignored and frustrated
yearning — a longing to live a more integrated life, to
experience non-fragmentation for a change,
to be at home in our own skin. Who doesn't long for
that kind of peace and well-being?

• • •

But hang on. While we may long for wholeness, the great irony is that it is already here in any and every moment, and it is already ours. If we could realize this — that is, make it real in our lives — it would amount to a profound "rotation in consciousness," a waking up to a deeper unity enveloping and permeating our whole life.

This rotation in consciousness *is* awareness. As we have already discussed, awareness allows us to see and to realize that we are seeing, to think and to know what's on our minds, and to experience emotion and be in relationship to it in a way that is actually wise and self-compassionate — that doesn't saddle us with stories of how great we are or how horrible we are or how inadequate we are. Such narratives can act like cement boots that sink us in a morass more or less of our own creation — that is, if we believe them, if we think they are the truth rather than recognizing them as merely thoughts coming and going.

This is not to say that meditation is suggesting that you "should" know who you are in any conventional and narrative sense of "knowing." It's much more a matter of asking whether you can even pose the question and pose it over and over again, and perhaps come to be comfortable with not knowing, or at least, at first, admitting to not knowing completely. People might ask, "Who are you?" And in response, of course, you might say "I'm Jon" or "I'm Katherine." But that is just a name that your parents gave you when you were born. They could have given you another name. If they had, would you still be the same person? Is it true that a rose by any other name would smell as sweet?

We might hold up the same prism to your age, your accomplishments, and everything else. None of it adds up to the person. The person is something else, something more mysterious, something bigger. Walt Whitman said, in "Song of Myself": "I am large! I contain multitudes!"

It's actually true. We are like universes, each one of us. We are boundless.

Paying Attention in a Different Way

Our true nature may be boundless. Still, we may be very much in the unconscious, unexamined habit of thinking of ourselves in small, contracted ways.

• • •

We may be very much bound up in identifying with the *contents* of our thoughts and emotions and with the narratives we build around ourselves based on how much we like or dislike what is happening to us. The power of mindfulness lies precisely in examining the fundamental elements of our lives — in particular all those self-identifications we indulge in and their consequences for ourselves and for others — and in examining the views and perspectives we adopt and then proceed to think are us.

The value of mindfulness lies in paying attention in a different, larger way, to the actuality of life unfolding moment by moment by moment. It lies in paying attention to the miracle and beauty of our very being and to the expanded possibilities for being, knowing, and doing within a life that is lived and met and held in greater awareness.

I call this an "orthogonal rotation in consciousness." Nothing is different, yet everything is different — because we have rotated in our way of seeing, our way of being, our way of knowing.

Not Knowing

Not knowing is not such a bad thing. As we have seen, it is the essence of a beginner's mind.

•••

Not knowing is basically just being honest about our ignorance. It is not shameful, although a lot of us think it is. Of course, we may be afraid to say in a group or in a class at school that we don't know something because we don't want to look foolish. We have been highly conditioned to feel that way. But consider this: all great scientists have to admit what they don't know and constantly keep it in mind. If they don't, they would never be in a position to discover anything meaningful because new discoveries and realizations happen at the interface between what is known and what is not known.

If you are completely preoccupied with what is already known, you can't make the leap into that other dimension of creativity or imagination or poetry, or whatever it is that allows for seeing a hidden order in things which, until it is seen and realized, it isn't seen at all.

The Prepared Mind

Perhaps you have had the
experience of somebody else seeing something that you missed,
even though you were in as good a position to see it. You might say,
"Why didn't I see that?"

• • •

Perhaps you weren't paying attention in quite the way that was required for the mind to be open to that particular realization in that moment. Perhaps it is because everybody has their own life trajectory and conditioning . . . the momentum behind them that tills the soil of their attention so it is or isn't available and receptive in any given moment. Louis Pasteur famously said: "Chance favors the prepared mind."

And what is the prepared mind? It is a ready mind, an open mind, a mind that knows or maybe just intuits what it doesn't know, questions its own tacit assumptions, and is drawn to inquire — to look more deeply beneath the appearance of things and perhaps behind the conventional narrative about why things are or aren't the way they are.

What Is Yours to See?

Maybe you can't see what is somebody else's to see. But maybe, just maybe, you can see what is yours to see. So what is yours to see?

• • •

This is a great question to ponder, to make your own, to let live inside your bones and your pores, and to guide your life. It may indeed be a lifetime's work to ask yourself this question and others such as: "What is my Way with a capital W?" "What is my Job with a capital J on the planet?" "What is my heart yearning for?" "What is my body really asking of me in this moment?" Even "Who is meditating?" Especially "Who is meditating?!"

You might then proceed to nurture those elements of your life as if that cultivation were really the only work worth doing on the planet. And you could make the argument that that is true. And that the responses to those questions might change over time, might ripen and mature.

Perhaps stillness will be a part of it. Perhaps silence. Perhaps taking action in a wholehearted way. For some, that calling might be in the service of the well-being of others, with actions that put others' interests before your own, as in the Hippocratic Oath that has been handed down by generation after generation of physicians from the time of Aesculapius and the ancient Greek roots of our Western culture.

PART III

DEEPENING

No Place to Go,
Nothing to Do

In many Asian languages,
the word for "mind" and the word for "heart" is the same word.
So when you hear the word "mindfulness," you have to hear
the word "heartfulness" simultaneously to understand or
feel what mindfulness really is.

● ● ●

That is why mindfulness is sometimes described as an *affectionate attention* and why I encourage you to approach the practice with a very light touch, bringing an attitude of gentleness and compassion to yourself at every turn.

Mindfulness is not some kind of cold, hard, clinical, or analytical witnessing, nor is it a pushing through to some special, more desirable state of mind, nor a sorting through the detritus and debris of the mind to discover the gold underneath. You can feel the *forcing, doing, striving* elements in this way of thinking about meditation and its potential benefits. It may help to remind ourselves over and over again that meditation is not about doing! It is about *being*, as in human being. It is about the *attending* itself, pure and simple.

As the Heart Sutra, a great text within the Mahayana Buddhist tradition, reminds us, there is "no place to go, nothing to do, nothing to attain."

The Doing That Comes Out of Being

In the early stages of meditation practice, you might find yourself wondering, "Well, if I adopt the attitude that there is 'no place to go, nothing to do, nothing to attain,' I will never make any progress with the practice or with anything else. With that attitude, I will never get anything done. But I have all sorts of things that I absolutely have to get done in my day and in my life.
I have responsibilities!

• • •

The fact of the matter is that meditation is not about navel-gazing or giving up functioning in the world. Nor is it about giving up engaging passionately in projects of real value and getting things done, nor will it make you stupid or rob you of ambition or motivation.

On the contrary, meditation is very much a way of letting all the doing you are engaged in and care about come out of being. Then, whatever emerges is something other than mere doing because it is informed by other dimensions of experience that come from intimately knowing your own mind. This intimacy develops through systematic cultivation, and that cultivation itself comes out of the discipline of attending. This is what we mean by the *practice* of mindfulness. It is the *how* of coming to our senses moment by moment. There really is no place to go in this moment. We are already here. Can we be here fully?

There really is nothing do to. Can we let go into non-doing, into pure being?

There really is nothing to attain, no special "state" or "feeling," because whatever you are experiencing in this moment is already special, already extraordinary, by virtue of the fact that it is being experienced.

The paradox of this invitation is that everything you might wish for is already here.

And the only important thing is to be the knowing that awareness already is.

To Act Appropriately

Mindfulness is required
to be able to see beneath the surface of appearances to what is
actually unfolding in your own experience,
in your own body, in your own mind.

• • •

Mindfulness is required to be able to hear what is really being said by a patient or a colleague or a friend, or by your child. Mindfulness is required to pick up on a look that flashes momentarily across somebody's face when you've said something hurtful but you don't quite realize what you actually said and how it was heard, and missed seeing that you shot an arrow, at least metaphorically, into the other person's heart—and you yourself are clueless about having done it.

Mindfulness can actually hold all of this in such a way that you might not shoot that arrow in the first place, but if you do, you'll see the effect of it and you'll have enough integrity and character to apologize and say, "I'm sorry I caused you harm" or "That must have hurt. Please forgive me."

If You Are Aware of What Is Happening, You Are Doing It Right

It is very common for people who begin the practice of mindfulness to wonder whether they are doing it right and whether what they are experiencing is what they should be experiencing.

• • •

My briefest response to the question, "Am I doing it right?" is that if you are aware of what is happening, you are "doing it right," no matter what is happening. That may be hard to accept, but it is true. What's more, it's all right to be experiencing what you are experiencing, even if you don't like it or it doesn't feel very "meditative." Actually it is perfect. It is the curriculum of the present moment, of your life unfolding here and now.

When you practice mindfulness, the first thing you are likely to notice is how mindless you can be. Let's say you decide to focus on the *feeling* of the breath moving in and out of the body. It is happening in the present moment. It is important. You can't live without breathing. It is not hard to locate the sensations in the body associated with breathing, at the belly or in the chest, or at the nostrils. You might find yourself saying, "What is the big deal? I will just keep my focus on the breath."

Well, lots of luck with that one. Because invariably, you will find that the mind has a life of its own and is not interested in taking orders from you about staying focused on the breath or anything else. So it is very likely that you will find your attention dissipating over and over again, forgetting about this breath in this moment, and being preoccupied with something else — anything else — in spite of your own best intentions. This is just part and parcel of the landscape of meditation practice, and it tells you something about the nature of your own mind.

Remember, we have established that the *objects* of attention are not of primary importance. What is of primary importance is the quality of the *attending* itself. So the mind's wanderings — its self-distractedness; its changeability; its dullness on occasion; its excitability; its endless proliferations, constructions, and projects; its lack of focus — are all telling you something important, even critically important, about your own mind. It is not that you are doing anything wrong. You are not! You are simply beginning to realize how little we actually know ourselves and our own minds.

This awareness is far more important than whether your attention in a particular moment is focused on the breath sensations or not. If we understand this, the mind's own distractedness and unreliability become new and worthy objects of attention in virtually every and any moment.

When your attention wanders away from the breath, it is not a mistake, and it doesn't mean that you are a bad meditator. It is just what happened in that moment. The important thing is that you noticed it. Can you let it in and be aware of it? Can you not add anything to it? This is where the non-judgmental piece comes in.

Non-Judging Is an Act of
Intelligence and Kindness

Iff you are going to
criticize yourself every time your mind wanders
out of the present moment, well, you're going to be
criticizing yourself a lot.

• • •

Maybe it is time to stop berating or belittling ourselves for not living up to some romantic "spiritual" ideal. How about just noticing what is unfolding? When we think we have "blown it completely" by forgetting about the breath altogether during a period of formal practice, how about just bringing awareness to thinking that you "blew it"? That thought is itself a judgment, just one more internal commentary. You haven't "blown" anything. There is nothing wrong with you. And there is nothing wrong with your mind. These are just judgments the mind is generating in reaction to one experience of your attention wandering away from its chosen object. You will have millions, billions of such moments. They don't matter, but they can teach us a lot. Can you see that you can dwell in awareness or come back to awareness, at least for brief moments, over and over again, even as the mind goes here and there and is preoccupied with this or that?

In each new moment, we are presented with this option, to see what is actually happening, which we call *discernment*, rather than to fall into judging, which is usually overly simplistic, dualistic, binary thinking: black or white, good or bad, either/or. Suspending judging, or not judging the judging that does arise, is an act of intelligence, not an act of stupidity. It is also an act of kindness toward yourself, as it runs counter to the tendency we all have to be so hard on ourselves, and so critical.

You Can Only Be Yourself—
Thank Goodness!

Awareness itself
is what mindfulness is about.

• • •

It is not about achieving an ideal, or a particularly desirable or longed-for special state.

If the mind is thinking: "If I meditate I'll always be compassionate, I'll be like the Dalai Lama, I'll be like Mother Teresa" or whoever your spiritual guru/hero of the moment is, it may help to remind yourself that you don't stand a snowball's chance in hell of being like the Dalai Lama or Mother Teresa or anybody else. Nor do you know what their interior experience is.

The only person that you have the remotest possibility of being like is yourself. And that, when it comes down to it, is the real challenge of mindfulness: the challenge to be yourself.

The irony, of course, is that you already are.

Embodied Knowing

What does it mean that we are already who we are? And how can we embody that knowing and be the essence of that knowing moment by moment?

• • •

How will we embody that knowing in the most stressful moments, when the proverbial stuff is hitting the proverbial fan?

What happens when we are overwhelmed by mind-states such as anxiety, boredom, impatience, irritability, sadness, despair, rage, jealousy, greed, elation, a sense of personal importance or lack of importance, or any of the myriad emotional reactions that we may be catapulted into on any given day by very real circumstances?

How do these breezes and sometimes storms in the mind relate to who we are in *that* moment? What are our choices in terms of being in wiser relationship to what is going on in the field of awareness — the weather patterns, the overhanging cloud cover, the turbulence that on occasion arise and dominate the mind and heart?

Life itself offers us unending opportunities to explore these often overlooked aspects of our own being. That would include cultivating greater intimacy with the range of what are sometimes called positive emotions, which are also part of the human repertoire and are not necessarily limited to pleasant or pleasing circumstances.

We might ask whether it is possible to inhabit a sense of well-being in any given moment, to experience a profound sense of flourishing, of what is sometimes called eudaemonia? We might explore the possible roles of joy, delight, empathy, or contentment in the full expression of our lives.

Might it be possible to be aware of fleeting moments of joy, perhaps in the absence of the storms and cloudiness that are also fleeting if we don't feed them? Perhaps joy or well-being is already here and we are ignoring it, or we don't have the proper lenses to even detect such currents in ourselves.

These innate capacities and qualities of heart and mind can be developed and expanded through the tender embrace that mindfulness in the present moment invites. When cultivated, they may be more available to us, even in times of great difficulty.

Feeling Joy for Others

Feelings of compassion and loving-kindness for others can be developed and refined.

• • •

Like joy and a sense of well-being, compassion for others and loving-kindness are currents native to our hearts and minds, and so are already present. Perhaps they are simply unattended and unobserved, obscured by the overgrown vegetation of our usually entangled minds, preoccupied as they often are with our endlessly driven agendas.

If we are on the lookout for them, feelings of compassion and loving-kindness for others can actually be recognized and welcomed into awareness, along with perhaps some compassion and loving-kindness directed toward ourselves. This is often the hardest part — recognizing anything within ourselves worthy of compassion. However, believe it or not, these qualities of the heart are all intimate denizens of our own interior landscape. While they may ordinarily go unnoticed and unexplored, that circumstance can change anytime we care to approach our experience in an openhearted and matter-of-fact way, just as an experiment.

Awareness might then serve as an open doorway into new ways of being in relationship to the full repertoire of our emotional life — without having to do any work at all or having to become a new or different kind of person.

The Full Catastrophe

So much of the time, we can find ourselves in pain in one way or another, suffering in the face of what Zorba the Greek called "the full catastrophe" of life — nothing less than the human condition itself — which often manifests in our lives in ways we may not feel we had "signed up for." But even in such moments, some other dimension of the experience may be available to us, especially if we notice that our awareness of the pain that we are experiencing isn't itself in pain.

• • •

Of course, this takes investigation and looking where we most don't want to look. That is one virtue of the cultivation of mindfulness and the intentionality behind the practice — to help us to turn toward that which we are most impelled to turn away from.

Is My Awareness of Suffering Suffering?

Y̤ou might ask yourself
at some point when you find yourself hurting:
"Is my awareness of my suffering suffering?"

• • •

You might try looking at what is arising in your experience in a moment of suffering and sustain the looking for a few moments longer than you feel comfortable with, as if you were dipping your toe in the water, with a light and gentle touch, but you're still determined to feel what is here and apprehend the quality of your awareness. With practice, you might try extending the exploration over longer periods, so that your investigation of what we identify as suffering has a chance to stabilize in awareness. It would be good to try this out on a number of different occasions. This is a way to befriend unpleasant and difficult experiences.

You could investigate anxiety in a moment of fear in a similar way by asking: "Is my awareness of my fear, my trepidation, my worry, my anxiety frightened?" and then looking deeply. Or, you could investigate a moment of pain by asking: "Is my awareness of the pain in pain?" Or, "Is my awareness of my sadness sad, my depression depressed, or my feeling worthless worthless?" Of course, it is best to do this when the feeling is strong, and not as a theoretical or conceptual exercise.

I am not saying that this is easy. Nor am I saying that it will magically make anything better. It's not supposed to. But it is a way to work with enormous pain and harm in potentially transformative and liberative ways.

As a next step, you might then experiment with dropping the "my" altogether and see how that feels, so that it is no longer *my* suffering, *my* anxiety, *my* sadness. In other words, letting go of the selfing, which simply means to be aware of it. Perhaps you are getting the sense that awareness can, in a moment, turn the tables on our deepest beliefs about our experience as we investigate the full extent of that experience, as opposed to merely living in a habitual reactivity colored and perpetuated by old, worn-out patterns of thought with little or no awareness.

What Does Liberation
from Suffering Mean?

Once, in Shenzhen, China, I met with a ninety-eight-year-old Chan Master who said to me when MBSR was explained to him: "There are an infinite number of ways in which people suffer. Therefore, there must be an infinite number of ways in which the Dharma is made available to people." What he meant by *Dharma* was the universal teachings of the Buddha on suffering and the possibility of liberation from suffering.

● ● ●

When the Buddha spoke of the Dharma as the path to the "liberation from suffering," he was referring to the suffering that we make for ourselves on top of the suffering that comes from natural and human events that are beyond our ability to control.

This "extra" suffering is called *adventitious suffering,* meaning "extrinsic rather than intrinsic," "out of place," or "accidental," from the Latin, *adventicius,* meaning "coming to us from abroad" and its root, *advenire,* "to arrive." In other words, it is not a given. It is this kind of suffering that we do not have to be imprisoned by, that we can do something about, that we can be entirely free of according to the Buddha, based on his meditative "laboratory investigations" of his own experience — and that of countless dharma practitioners since. And when we investigate for ourselves, through our own systematic cultivation of mindfulness in the face of the very particular and personal pain that we may be suffering at one time or another (the word "suffering" comes from the Latin, *sufferre,* the root meaning of which is "to carry or to bear"), we can see that much of it is indeed a form of suffering that we create for ourselves on top of what the outer circumstances bring us, which can be horrific enough without our compounding it.

It is adventitious suffering that causes us by far the vast majority of the suffering we experience. Pain of all kinds — physical, emotional, social, existential, spiritual — is a part of the human condition and so, inevitable at times. The cliché is that while pain may be inevitable, the suffering that accompanies it is optional. What this means is that *how we choose to be in relationship to pain makes an enormous difference.*

We can see that liberation from suffering does not mean that we get a free pass out of all suffering just by practicing mindfulness. If you are human, you are going to suffer at times. It is part of the human condition. It is inescapable. Just having a body is a prescription for suffering. Just having a mind that doesn't know itself is a prescription for suffering. As we have seen, being attached to anything, clinging to anything, is a prescription for suffering. So we will suffer. You might also contribute to the suffering of others, sometimes without even knowing it. The question is, is it possible to investigate and befriend our suffering no matter what the circumstances? Are there commonsensical and practical ways for us to approach deeply painful experiences and not make them worse? What might be the consequences of seeing that it is possible to intentionally and mindfully *work with* pain and suffering when they do arise in our lives?

Hell Realms

In any moment, countless
people all over the planet are caught in one hell realm or another,
one aspect or another of the full catastrophe. It is not to be minimized.
The suffering is enormous. And a great deal of it is not adventitious.

• • •

Sometimes suffering is because of war or other forms of violence; because of loss, grief, humiliation, shame, a sense of powerlessness or worthlessness; or from being in prison or imprisoned by addictions and blindness. These hell realms themselves can compound violence, sometimes leading people to do terrible things to themselves or to others.

And yet, in the face of even the most unthinkably terrifying situations, we have a powerful innate capacity to hold whatever it is — even terror, despair, and rage — in awareness, and carry it differently. We can see this in the many different acts of kindness that occur even in times of war and hardship. As humans, we can meet and carry our hurt, our anger, our fear in new ways that can be deeply restorative and healing.

This is what mindfulness as a practice offers us: a new way of being in relationship to what is, not as an escape route or as an expedient, but as a way of being more in touch with our humanity, our goodness, and our beauty.

Moreover, in the poignancy — or even the horror — of any moment, we can recognize through having seen it over and over again in the mindfulness practice itself what is sometimes called the law of impermanence: the fact that everything, without exception, is always changing, that things will not, cannot stay the same forever. In the present moment, we can also recognize that our awareness is already free — even in prison, even in hell — and gives us the freedom to choose how to respond inwardly to our circumstances, even if our outer circumstances are beyond our control. Viktor Frankl put it this way in his book, *Man's Search for Meaning,* describing his experience in a Nazi concentration camp: "Everything can be taken from a human being but one thing: the last of the human freedoms — to choose one's attitude in any given set of circumstances, to choose one's own way."

Liberation Is in the Practice Itself

A mountain climber in the high Andes, after having fallen because his climbing partner felt he had no alternative but to cut the rope between them or lose his own life, had no options left to him except to go down into an ice crevice, trailing a severely broken and painful leg. With his life in the balance, there was no possibility of going in the direction he most wanted to go to survive — up. His only option at that point was to descend into the dark and hope he would emerge in a place where he could find a way out and to safety.

• • •

Similarly, there may be times when we too have no choice but to go further into the dark and persevere through the horror, the suffering — with perhaps not even a glimmer of any realistic "solution" or end to any of it on the horizon. There is simply no alternative. But how we go into it makes a huge difference. In his case, miraculously, the climber found a way out and survived.

When we suffer, the poignancy of the circumstances always has a sense of uniqueness to it. And for good reason. Whatever is happening is happening to us, not to somebody else. It is always accompanied by a story as we try desperately to explain the unexplainable to ourselves. Suffering can suddenly arise, in any of its infinite manifestations, unexpectedly in the middle of our very rich and textured lives and relationships, hopes and dreams, histories and unfinished business. It may signal the end of something, it may signal irreparable loss. Events can dash all hopes and dreams in an instant, rend the fabric of our lives, turn everything upside down, and destroy what is most beautiful and loveable. There is no denying this.

What the practice of mindfulness offers us is a way to be in relationship to this enormity, to this poignancy, and to the particulars of the narrative — even when it seems impossible for us or anyone else to do anything. It invites us to be willing, over and over again in the face of even our own overwhelm, reluctance, and despair, to turn *toward* what we most want to turn away from. It invites us to accept what seems beyond accepting and to experiment with embracing the actuality of it with a sense of enormous kindness toward ourselves. This is a practice — one that can only unfold over time.

We embrace what is occuring in awareness and acceptance because we have no viable and intelligent alternative. And we embrace it not as a form of passive resignation or surrender, as we have seen, but as a way of being in wiser relationship to what is, to what has been, and to the unknowableness of what will unfold. And we undertake it only within our capacity of any moment.

There is strength in this. There is a quiet dignity in this. And it is not contrived. It is not forced. It is not a romantic idealization of a special state of being. It is not the enacting of a method or a technique. It is not the implementation of a philosophy. It is one human being or a group of people or a society standing in full awareness in the poignancy of what is. This is what the *practice* of mindfulness actually cultivates: a willingness to rest in the not knowing, in the awareness of both knowing and not knowing, and respond appropriately to whatever it is that needs attending to in this moment, within the circumstances we find ourselves, with kindness toward oneself and toward those who most need our tenderness and our clarity.

Herein lies liberation from suffering. The liberation is in the practice itself, and in each moment when we can take refuge in the domain of not knowing. Out of such moments, we can take action even in the face of loud interior narratives that predict hopelessness, despair, and failure. Even in the moments when we do lose our mind and our heart, in the next moment or whenever we are ready, we can begin again, and again, and again. We can return over and over to something deep within ourselves that is steady, that is reliable, that is whole — and that is not a thing.

The Beauty of the Mind That Knows Itself

We could say that all of the greatest works of art and culture and science, the contents of museums and libraries throughout the world, and what unfolds in concert halls and between the covers of great works of literature and poetry, stem from the human mind that knows itself to one degree or another or that is at least interested in exploring the interface between knowing and not-knowing.

• • •

On the other hand, throughout human history, all of the most horrific atrocities and horrors that one person or group or nation or tribe has perpetrated on another or on itself also stems from that same human mind when it does *not* know itself, when it refuses to look at itself in relationship to the whole, and actively (and often cynically) chooses narrowly defined self-interest, greed, animosity, delusion, violence, and mindlessness over awareness, mindfulness, and the sense of interconnectedness, cooperativity, and kindness that naturally unfolds from a more mindful and heartful way of seeing, knowing, and being in the world.

As we have seen, we have countless opportunities to step out of the well-worn story-line of our thinking and of getting hijacked by our emotions and our ideas and opinions, our likes and dislikes, and instead, to rest in awareness.

Our own awareness has the capacity to free us, at least for one time-less moment, from the toxic elements of thought and emotion and the habit-driven suffering that usually arises from them when they are unmet, unexamined, and unwelcomed in awareness.

Taking Care of Your Meditation Practice

Meditation is the cultivation of
that gesture of welcoming unflinchingly whatever arises —
of welcoming it wholeheartedly into awareness.

• • •

Cultivation (*bhavana* in Pali) is an agricultural term: it conjures the planting of seeds, the watering of those seeds, and then the protecting of them to give them time to grow. And you do have to protect them, because they'll get eaten by the birds, or trampled by the cows, or washed away by the rain. That is why there are fences and drainage ditches around fields and young orchards and vineyards.

With the seed of mindfulness, we are talking of a potential that resembles an acorn that, if watered regularly and protected in the early stages, is capable of growing into a towering and sheltering oak whose branches and foliage can provide dependable refuge from the elements.

So it makes sense to take care of your nascent meditation practice, especially for the first thirty or forty years. It is precious and can easily be trampled or washed away by all the competing demands of the day and of your own mind.

Energy Conservation in
Meditation Practice

Iff you are just starting
out, it helps to be on the lookout for the natural
impulse to talk with other people about your
meditation practice or to casually mention that
you are beginning to meditate.

• • •

It is easy to dissipate your energy in this way. If someone doesn't respond positively to what you are sharing with them or slights the idea of meditation in any way, even unintentionally, you may become discouraged before you even get started or build enough constancy into your practice so that other people's opinions don't matter to you in this regard.

Also, if you wax enthusiastic about your meditation practice and how great it is, and this becomes a habit, pretty soon you may be wasting what little energy you have talking about your meditation "experience" and how great your "insights" are, and how wonderful and transformative mindfulness is, rather than practicing. The risk is that pretty soon you won't have any time to meditate any more; you will have become more involved with the story of your meditation practice than with the ongoing experience of meditating. This, of course, is more selfing manifesting itself, only now it is being built around the subject of mindfulness. It is endlessly amazing what the mind will do to construct and reinforce an identity.

For this and other reasons, it would be useful to bring some care and attention and intentionality to whom you feel impelled to speak with about your meditation practice and to what you wind up saying. It can be very helpful to have at least one person — hopefully someone who is also practicing and who is more experienced than you are, or who at least has been at it longer — with whom you can talk about your practice in some detail. But other than that, it is probably best to minimize how much you talk about it with others beyond just explaining what you need to to family and friends who might be interested. That way, you won't waste the nascent energies you are mobilizing that are necessary to keep up the momentum of formal practice through thick and thin. In a sense, you are reinvesting those energies, pouring them back into the practice itself and into your growing relationship with silence and non-doing.

You are letting how you live, your actions and attitudes, speak for you with no need to synthesize a satisfying narrative for others, or even for yourself.

An Attitude of Non-Harming

There is an ethical
foundation to the cultivation of mindfulness. Mindfulness
is an orientation to reality that is highly connected with compassion,
starting with yourself. It is based above all on the principle of
non-harming, or *ahimsa* (in Sanskrit).

• • •

In every moment, the invitation is to be present with and for yourself as you are, with an attitude of openness, generosity, and kindness. As we have seen, being non-judgmental means that it is important not to criticize yourself every time you don't live up to your own self-created, usually unrealistic standards. To berate yourself in such a way would hardly be consistent with the spirit of non-harming.

When we intentionally align ourselves with non-harming as the core motivation and foundation of mindfulness practice, it allows us to take an entirely different perspective on how we might be in relationship to our various transitory but often painful states of mind, as well as to the whole of our lives as they unfold moment by moment, and even to the question of what our deepest and most important needs might be.

Non-harming lies at the core of the Hippocratic Oath in medicine— *"Primum non nocere"*: "First, do no harm." It is a vow that doctors take when they formally enter the profession after training. If you cultivate that kind of attitude toward yourself, then when you take your seat on a chair or on a meditation cushion you can rest in awareness with ease, without having to get anywhere else, or experience anything special.

Because as we have seen, this moment is already special.

Greed:
The Cascade of Dissatisfactions

The Buddhists have a very down-to-earth way of talking about certain unhealthy and potentially destructive mind states. They simply refer to them as *poisons*. These toxic mind states, as they are also called, are grouped into three categories.

• • •

The first poison is that of greed. Greed is the impulse to acquire whatever it is that you desire. To call that "toxic" may sound a bit on the strong side, but when you come right down to it, it is a very useful lens to hold up to our own behavior so that we can bring greater awareness to our impulses and our actions and to their very real consequences.

We are constantly grasping at things we want. Sometimes it is just a little greediness — we want more food, or more credit, or more love. And sometimes it's a large hunger that cannot be satisfied, no matter how hard we try. But little or big, if we don't get the object of our immediate desire, we can feel incomplete, out of sorts, perhaps totally miserable.

Of course, we sincerely believe that if we just get that one thing we are lacking, whatever it is, then we will feel complete again. And that is true, as far as it goes. It does feel good . . . until we feel incomplete again, and then we grasp a little bit more . . . until we get the next thing. And that sets off a never-ending cascade of dissatisfactions. It is clinging writ large, the tendency that the Buddha declared to be the root cause of suffering. When greed is operating, there always seems to be something missing — something that if only we had it, we would be complete.

We all recognize this pattern, but we can often see it much more clearly in other people than we can in ourselves. That doesn't mean that we cannot desire things or that we should not have goals or ambitions. It simply reminds us that we generate less suffering in ourselves and others when we are aware of how attached we may be to our desires and then let that awareness modulate our thoughts, emotions, and actions.

This is easy to say, not so easy to live.

Aversion:
The Flip Side of Greed

Hatred or aversion
is the flip side of greed. It too arises from our unexamined
attachment to our desire — only now it is the desire that
things be different from how they are.

• • •

Aversion arises from anything you don't want or don't like, that you want to run away from, that you recoil from, that you wish to push away or have disappear. Anything unwanted is lumped under this one category: aversion. Aversion lies at the heart of many big emotions — anger, hatred, rage, fear — and also smaller emotions such as irritability, resentment, grumpiness, annoyance.

It can be enormously revealing to experiment with noticing in yourself how many times during the day aversion rears its head in one way or another: a twinge of annoyance at how someone says something, or loads the dishwasher in a way that is not your way, or stores a tool upside down that obviously, at least to your way of thinking, needs to be cared for in the exact opposite way; or when the weather is not to your liking; or when somebody accuses you of doing something (even something minor or trivial) that you actually didn't do, or of not taking care of something that you actually did take care of; or when you are not given credit by people whose opinions you care about for something meritorious that you did.

Occasions that reliably trigger aversive contraction in us are manna from heaven if you are ready for them. They afford infinite, if humbling, occasions for seeing how much what we think is our true well-being depends on having our own way, for seeing how strongly and unconsciously attached we are to wanting things to unfold as we want them to unfold, and for wanting to be treated as if everybody in the world knew exactly how we wanted and needed to be treated.

You can feel the seething tide of selfing in these examples and how toxic the internal narrative can become. And no doubt you can feel it in those myriad examples that are probably flooding into your own mind as you reflect on how you are in relationship to the arising of anything and everything you don't like, however trivial, and how very personally you take it all.

In this way, mindfulness of aversion is profoundly healing, because it offers us a way to at least momentarily dissolve the self-imposed but unconscious straightjacket of such automatic and unconscious reactions. A modicum of awareness, even after the fact, allows us to see that we have very real choices in such moments. It reminds us that we do not have to be a perpetual prisoner of aversion if we reflect on what just unfolded and whether we really are better off for our emotional reaction. It also signals us that at the next opportunity, which is usually right around the corner, we can remember to see more clearly and let ourselves feel in the body the contractive energies arising from not having things happen as we would like them to. In this way, we can consciously choose to let the turbulent energies of that moment arise, do their complex thing, and pass away much like the smoke patterns ascending from an extinguished candle, without taking any of it personally or having to control what is unfolding through forcing of any kind.

That does not mean that we will not act forcefully in the face of harmful and threatening circumstances. Taking principled and brave stands in the face of harmful and threatening circumstances is an intimate part of living a life of integrity, wakefulness, and caring. Indeed, depending on the circumstances, it might be a necessary enactment and an embodiment of our clarity, our wisdom, and our compassion.

But then it would no longer be personal in any small sense. Instead, it becomes a manifestation of our wholeness and a natural extension of our practice of no separation.

Delusion and the Trap of
Self-Fulfilling Prophecies

The third poison, delusion,
is the exact opposite of wisdom. It is not seeing things
as they actually are. It also goes by the name *illusion*.

• • •

Both delusion and illusion arise from not apprehending and comprehending with clarity the relationships among different and often complex events and things, and therefore not realizing what is actually going on. Instead, we are living inside our own little narrative bubble of the moment, frequently misattributing cause and effect and therefore completely imprisoned in thoughts and emotions that are both inaccurate and misguided.

Too often our unexamined and deluded story-lines become self-fulfilling prophecies. We can always marshal any evidence we want in support of a particular view, and then believe it even if it is patently not true. This is delusion. We see a great deal of this writ large in the political and social landscape.

Now Is Always the Right Time

Between greed, hatred, and delusion, there's a lot to pay attention to. And we can begin very close to home. We don't have to criticize anybody else, nor do we have to criticize ourselves or take any of it personally.

● ● ●

The whole point is simply to see the play of these various mind-states and their effects on the body and how it actually feels moment by moment. As we have seen, there is a lot to be aware of, and that is why mindfulness packs so much transformative power, so much healing power, such a capacity for orienting us and helping us to grow into ourselves.

This capacity is present and accessible across the entire life-span. It doesn't matter how old you are when you discover mindfulness practice or when you first heard the word "mindfulness" and decided that you felt some affinity and attraction to its promise as a practice. It doesn't matter because, basically, it is the promise of reclaiming your life, or more accurately, of giving your life back to yourself. That can happen at any age, and in any moment.

Now is always the right time because it is the only time. Just check your watch or clock.

Unbelievable!

How does it happen?

It is now again.

The "Curriculum" Is "Just This"

Not only is it always now. The "curriculum" of this adventure we call living, where mindfulness can play such a pivotal role, is always what is unfolding in this moment, whether we like what is happening or not.

• • •

Whatever is arising in this moment becomes the curriculum for liberating ourselves from the shackles of greed, hatred, and delusion. We do not need some ideal or romantic fairy tale of what would be best for us. What we most need is what is already given to us: the actuality of things as they are in the only moment we will ever have — this one.

And the key for apprehending and comprehending what is happening and for liberating ourselves from the momentum of our unconscious habits of mind lies in whether we can catch the moment in which it first registers that whatever has arisen is pleasant (if it is pleasant), or unpleasant (if it is unpleasant), or neither pleasant nor unpleasant. This is the basic and primary lens through which we apprehend any and every object of attention. It makes all the difference as to what happens in the very next moment in our mind and in our life — if we can be aware of this usually unconscious and automatic appraisal mechanism.

The definition of "pleasant" is that we desire our connection to the object of attention to be sustained, and we would suffer if it were curtailed. We want more of it, and we therefore can fall easily into greed in that moment if we do not simply note the pleasant quality in awareness and let it rest at that.

The definition of "unpleasant" is that we desire the experience of this moment to end, and would suffer if it were sustained. If we automatically fall into pushing it away or trying to shorten its duration, we have already fallen into aversion.

And the definition of "neither pleasant nor unpleasant" is that it has none of these attributes and is therefore hard to notice in the first place. When something is neither pleasant nor unpleasant, it is easy to ignore and we can therefore easily fall into delusion, ignorance, and illusion in relationship to it.

So mindfulness of the pleasant, unpleasant, or neutral quality of any moment is the key to not falling into the grip of greed, aversion, or delusion — or extracting ourselves rapidly when we do, as we inevitably will over and over again. Mindfulness, applied at the moment of contact with a particular object of attention arising in our experience, puts a momentary end to unnecessary, adventitious suffering, because the suffering resides neither in the unpleasantness nor in the pleasantness. It is in the aversion and in the greed — it is in the clinging and the self-identification.

All this can dissolve in a moment, when awareness apprehends what is actually unfolding . . . like the soap bubble being touched by the finger.

Liberation from suffering in that very moment.

Liberation from greed, hatred, and delusion.

Now for the next moment, which, of course, is this one.

Giving Your Life Back to Yourself

In the Stress Reduction Clinic, many of our patients say to us, with great regularity, that they feel that mindfulness training in the form of MBSR gave them back their lives and they are grateful to us for it.

• • •

We often point out that while that may be true to a degree, it is also true — perhaps even more true — that we didn't give them anything. Whatever benefits they received came from their own hard work with the meditation practice, from the inspiration and support of the other people in their class, from their own willingness to engage in and sustain mindfulness practice as a discipline over time, and from the fact of their already being whole in the first place.

The flowering of mindfulness in one's life is always more of a development and an integration of what is already here rather than an adding or subtracting of specific qualities. For our patients in the Stress Reduction Clinic, mindfulness is not a nice little idea that you pull out every time you feel stressed. Nor is it a relaxation technique. It's not a technique at all. It is a way of being.

So even though there are hundreds, if not thousands, of different meditation techniques, meditation isn't really about techniques at all.

The techniques, when understood and used properly, are simply skillful means for waking up to the actuality of what is already here and providing a more skillful — that is, wiser — way of being in relationship with it.

Bringing Mindfulness Further
into the World

Once you have established a foundation in formal practice and in allowing life itself to be both the real teacher and the real practice, you may discover that your natural creativity and imagination find many ways to carry the practice of mindfulness into different areas of life.

• • •

If you are a teacher, you may realize that it could be beneficial to teach your students the *how* of paying attention and to encourage them to cultivate greater awareness of the body, of their thoughts, and of their emotions both in the classroom and at home. You could think of it as teaching them to tune their instrument (of learning, creativity, and social connectedness) before expecting it to work optimally when they play it. This tuning and the actual playing that arises from it in all the forms that learning and inquiry, investigation and imagination take, reinforce each other over days, weeks, months, years, and indeed, an entire lifetime. The music keeps getting richer.

Exposure to mindfulness training by a skilled teacher can nurture greater emotional balance and intelligence in children, adolescents, and young adults. It can foster greater stress resilience and greater social intelligence and cooperativity — just what one would hope for from an enlightened and engaged citizenry. Many college professors are developing innovative curricula that incorporate mindfulness practice as a "laboratory" requirement and that investigate traditions of contemplative practice and their creative applications across a very wide range of disciplines in the humanities and in the sciences.

So if you are a teacher at any level, from preschool through graduate school, mindfulness may be a valuable ally in so many different aspects of your work and calling. It may also satisfy something deep within yourself that hungers for authenticity, connectivity, and a creativity that emerges as more than the sum of its individual components. It is profoundly satisfying indeed to feel the love of learning and a sense of adventure in discovery come alive in the classroom and see it manifest in your students' work and lives through the cultivation of mindfulness. As teachers, we live for this.

For similar reasons, mindfulness could be an ally in virtually any profession. Very few performance-based jobs would not benefit from greater awareness brought to the critical elements that lead to optimal productivity and staff satisfaction. Training in mindfulness is now being used by Fortune 100 and Fortune 500 companies to optimize performance in team-based projects, and to catalyze embodied leadership, innovation, creativity, emotional intelligence, and effective communication.

The military is also making use of mindfulness training to deal with the huge social costs of multiple deployments on troops and families, as well as to refine training that instills in soldiers greater stress resilience and greater discernment and restraint in counter-insurgency situations. This training is in part to hopefully dramatically reduce civilian casualties during combat operations in which the enemy doesn't wear uniforms, civilians are everywhere, and the soldiers themselves might be terrified.

Presumably mindfulness could be of profound use in the political process, where the intrinsically toxic forces of greed, aversion, delusion, and selfing often hold sway and may all too often obliterate any good intentions, intrinsic wisdom, integrity, and civility that may have originally inspired our political office holders to try to make a creative contribution to the well-being and betterment of our country.

Closer to home, bringing mindfulness to one's parenting — whether with newborns and small children, or with older children — can provide a vast and powerful universe of options for nurturing our children while continuing to develop and grow in our lives ourselves. The same can be said for mindful childbirth, mindful care of the elderly, mindfulness brought to the domain of sports and recreation, and mindfulness in the domain of the law and other social institutions.

So whatever your work, whatever your passions in life, you may find that mindfulness shows you new ways to enhance and optimize both your effectiveness and your enthusiasm for your work, ways that feed your innate creativity and fulfill your need for satisfying human relationships based on authenticity and good will. Those impulses — if brought to fruition through deep reflection and ongoing cultivation through practice and experimentation — can transform the world in ways little and big. In that sense, every single one of us is an agent of wisdom and transformation, of insight and healing, of creativity and imagination in this inter-embedded network we call humanity.

We have, in our brief lifetimes, all the moments we need to take responsibility for how we choose to be in relationship to what is and to what might be if we follow our hearts and our intrinsic wisdom. This opportunity invites us all to engage wholeheartedly, each in our own way, in an ongoing adventuring in the domain of the possible and the not yet realized.

PART IV

RIPENING

The Attitudinal Foundations of Mindfulness Practice

In addition to the ethical foundation on which mindfulness practice rests, there is also a complementary attitudinal foundation.

• • •

I have been alluding to it all along when speaking of the affectionate quality of attention and the need for being gentle and non-judgmental with ourselves. There are many more than seven, but these seven attitudes are fundamental. The others — including generosity, gratitude, forbearance, forgiveness, kindness, compassion, empathic joy, and equanimity — develop through the cultivation of these seven: non-judging, patience, beginner's mind, trust, non-striving, acceptance, and letting go.

1. NON-JUDGING

We've already seen why a non-judging attitude is so important if we are to see past the automatic and usually unexamined ideas and opinions we have about pretty much everything. When you begin paying attention to what's on your mind, you rapidly discover that basically everything is a judgment of one kind or another. It is good to be aware of this. No need to judge the judging or try to change it. Just seeing it is enough. Then true discernment can arise, a seeing things as they are. Not-knowing is akin to not judging. When we don't have to immediately know everything, we can be open to seeing with fresh eyes.

So when you begin to practice the guided meditations, notice how frequently judgments of various kinds arise. You only need to recognize them.

2. PATIENCE

We are always trying to get someplace else. We have a strong need to be on the way to some better moment, some better time when it all will come together for *me*. We can so easily become impatient and driven. Of course, this prevents us from being where we already are. The classic example is the child who wants to make the butterfly come out of the chrysalis sooner because it would be so nice to have the butterfly. So he just innocently peels apart the chrysalis, without any understanding that things unfold in their own time.

Patience is really a wonderful attitude to bring to mindfulness practice because the practice of mindfulness is already, in some fundamental sense, about stepping out of time altogether. When we are talking about the present moment, we are talking about now; we are talking about "outside of clock time." We've all had moments like that. In fact, we have nothing but moments like that, but we ignore almost all of them, and it's just once in a blue moon that we will experience a moment when time stops for us.

But actually, we can *learn* how to step out of clock time, how to drop into the timeless quality of now through the practice of mindfulness itself. This can give us a lot more time in our lives. Why? Because when we are mindful and inhabit each moment, we have, to a first approximation, an infinite number of them between now and the time we're going to die. That is a lot of time for living. So there is no hurry, and we can remind ourselves of this periodically and thereby embody greater patience.

3. BEGINNER'S MIND

We've already touched on the value of this attitude. We may need to call upon our beginner's mind over and over and over again, moment by moment, because our ideas and opinions and our expertise so easily cloud our ability to recognize what we don't know. As we've seen, resting in the awareness of *not knowing* is incredibly important in seeing with any clarity, with any creativity, and for living with integrity.

In your very first encounter with this book and CD, you may have still had a beginner's mind. But somewhere along the way, and it is pretty much inevitable, you may lose your beginner's mind for a time.

Perhaps with continued practice and reading, you will come to think you know something about meditation. If that occurs, you have probably already lost your beginner's mind momentarily. So it may be wiser to keep in mind how little anybody really knows about meditation. If you meet senior monks or nuns, even high lamas in the Tibetan tradition, or monastics and teachers — men and women — in other traditions, they will invariably tell you that they know very little. They typically display great humility and modesty. They might say, "You should really be studying with somebody else." Lamas with decades and decades of meditation training and practice and teaching may say, "I don't really know anything." And they're not joking, it's not false modesty — it's a signature of a beginner's mind. One Zen Master is famous for having described his forty years of teaching as "selling water by the river."

Beginner's mind is an attitude. It doesn't mean you don't know anything. It means that you are spacious enough in that moment to not be caught by what it is that you do know or have experienced in the face of the enormity of what is unknown.

If you think about the beauty and joyfulness of young children, some of that comes out of the freshness of beginner's mind. The challenge for us as adults is to see whether we can meet each moment and recognize it as fresh and therefore interesting — after all, we've never seen this one before. If you take a "you've seen one moment — or one breath — you've seen them all" attitude, you're going to get very bored cultivating mindfulness. Of course, even that doesn't have to be the end of the journey. You can just be aware of how bored you are watching your breath or your thoughts, for instance. And as we have seen, in that awareness you can ask yourself, "Is my awareness of my boredom bored?" If you investigate carefully, the answer will likely be, "Not at all." Your awareness isn't caught by your boredom.

In fact, with the attitude of beginner's mind, boredom can become unbelievably interesting. As you watch it, you might find that it dissolves into something much more interesting, another mind-state. That is equally true for virtually every mind-state, including the ones that we feel completely tyrannized by or are so terrified of that we don't even acknowledge to ourselves that we experience them: "Who me? Frightened? Scared? Tense? Not me." Can you hear the story of "not me"? That's the story of "me."

4. TRUST

The fourth attitudinal foundation of mindfulness is trust. Again, this is not some dime-store, goody-two-shoes notion of trust. We can ask: What is worthy of trust? Can we trust what we know? Can we trust what we know we don't know? Can we trust that things unfold in their own time and that we do not have to fix everything or even anything? Can we trust our own intuition in the face of contradiction by others? Can we trust that we are our own person?

On another note, can you trust what you think? Can you trust your ideas and opinions? Often they are unreliable because it is so easy for us to misperceive, misapprehend, mis-take what is actually going on. Maybe what you think is true is only true to a degree. Could that be so? Might it not be that we can be blinded to new possibilities by the unexamined assumption that our view is absolutely true?

If you can't entirely trust what you think, what about trusting awareness? What about trusting your heart? What about trusting your motivation to at least do no harm? What about trusting your experience until it's proven to be inaccurate — and then trusting *that* discovery?

What about trusting your senses? As you know, every sense can be tricked. So we may not be able to place an absolute trust in the senses, or in appearances. Still, perhaps we could experiment with training ourselves to be somewhat more in touch with the senses and see if we can develop a greater intimacy with what they reveal if we are attuned to them. This, of course, is akin to trusting the body.

Can you trust your body? Do you trust your body? What if your body had cancer in the past or has cancer now? Is there still room to find trust? Is there a sense that there might still be much more right with it than wrong with it — no matter what is wrong? Perhaps your attitudinal orientation can mobilize what is right with your body to live life as fully as possible while not knowing what is going to happen. Can we trust that not knowing? Sometimes yes, perhaps; sometimes no, sometimes we don't know. That "don't know" might itself be something you can trust.

5. NON-STRIVING

The fifth attitudinal foundation — this is a real kicker for Americans — is non-striving. Non-striving? What are you talking about? This sounds really subversive, even un-American. We are the proverbial go-getters, mega-doers. We could re-name our species "human doers." As a culture, we are really into doing, making progress, and always needing to get somewhere. So as we have already seen, the notion that in meditation practice there is no place to go, nothing to do, and nothing to attain can be quite strange and mysterious — even foreign — to our striving temperaments and our need to always be getting better.

Non-striving is related to the timeless quality of the present moment we call now. When we inhabit the present moment in the formal practice of meditation, there really, really, really is no place to go, nothing to do, and nothing to attain. Meditation is not like anything else you've ever taken on, such as learning to drive a car, where once you learn it, it becomes automatic, a skill that you use and never think about. That may be why there are fifty thousand fatal traffic accidents in the United States every year. At any given moment, perhaps the majority of us drivers are off someplace else, hardly in the car at all. We may be driving around but not really paying attention, maybe absorbed to one degree or another in a cell-phone conversation or what we are hearing on the radio. And even if you are not on the phone or distracted in some other way, well, in a sense the mind is often lost in thought, talking to itself. So perhaps if it is you behind the wheel, it would be a good idea to give yourself a call — via your internal "mindfulness network" — and remind yourself to stay in touch with what is unfolding out the windshield in front of you moment by moment.

Non-striving is not trivial. It involves realizing that you are already here. There's no place to go, because the agenda is simply to be awake. It is not framed as some ideal that suggests that after forty years of sitting in a cave in the Himalayas, or by studying with august teachers, or doing ten thousand prostrations, or whatever it is, you will necessarily be any better than you are now. It is likely that you will just be older. What happens now is what matters. If you don't pay attention now, as Kabir, the great Indian poet of sixteenth-century India, said, "You will simply end up with an apartment in the City of Death." T. S. Eliot put it this way in "Four Quartets," his last and greatest poem: "Ridiculous the waste sad time / Stretching before and after."

Even the tiniest little bit of reminding ourselves that "this is it," that we are alive now, that we are already here, can make a huge difference. For in fact, as we have seen, the future that we desire to get to — it is already here. This is it! This moment is the future of all the previous moments in your life, including those in which you thought about and dreamed of a future time. You are already in it. It is called "now." How you are in relationship to this moment influences the quality and character of the next moment. In this way, we can shape the future by taking care of the present. What a remarkable opportunity.

What is the purpose of living? Is it only to get someplace else and then when you're there realize that you are still not happy and you now want to be someplace else? If we are not careful, it may always seem like there is some better time over the horizon: "when I retire, when I graduate from high school or college, when I make enough money, when I get married, when I get divorced, when the kids move out." Wait a minute . . . This is it! This really is your life. You only have this moment. All the rest is memory (which is also here now) and anticipation (which is also happening here and now). This moment is as good as any other. In fact, it's perfect. Perfectly what it is. And this includes everything that you might think of as its imperfections.

As we've seen, non-striving certainly doesn't mean you don't know how to get a lot done. Many long-term meditators manage to get a great deal of excellent and important work done in the world in a variety of ways and venues, in every conceivable job and calling. The challenge for all of us is whether our doing is coming out of being, at least to some degree. That is an art form all its own: the art of conscious or mindful living. Again, as we've already seen, life itself becomes the true meditation practice.

This is not to idealize the practice. It is very real and often messy. It is not about attaining some special state of bliss or quietude. It is perpetually challenging us, always revealing new and more subtle areas of self-identification and clinging, just like life itself. It is hard.

However, the alternative to mindfulness is likely to be a lot harder, and a lot more problematic. At least intending to live mindfully offers a chance, renewable in every moment, for greater emotional balance, greater cognitive balance, and greater clarity of mind and heart. It is also a form of relational intelligence and therefore, to the degree that we embody it, we are less trying for those who live with us or around us.

6. ACCEPTANCE

This brings us to the sixth attitudinal foundation, acceptance. This one is very easily misunderstood. People might think that it means that whatever happens, they should "just accept it." No one is saying, "Just accept it." As we have seen, especially with horrific occurrences and circumstances, coming to acceptance is one of the hardest things in the world. Ultimately, it means realizing how things are and finding ways to be in wise relationship with them. And then to act, as appropriate, out of that clarity of vision.

Acceptance has nothing to do with passive resignation — far from it. If things are going to hell in a handbasket, then that knowing — that awareness — of things going to hell in a handbasket can give you a place to stand, an orientation for taking appropriate action in the next moment. But if you don't see and accept things as they actually are, you won't know how to act. Or you might be overwhelmed by fear, and that fear might cloud the mind just when you most need clarity and equanimity, or at least, if clarity and equanimity seem elusive, just when you need to be aware of the fear so that you can find ways to work with it rather than have it work against you. So acceptance is a whole universe in and of itself, and really a lifetime's engagement.

Let's say you have a chronic back condition and you're continually saying to yourself, "My life is over." Perhaps you are looking back to a time before you had the chronic back condition and thinking, "This has ruined my life." It may all be true to a degree, but can you see that this attitude closes down options for both the present and the future? Can you see that it makes for a very small story that you can easily become trapped in and that could readily lead to depression and despair — a story that could feed on itself and perpetuate itself, going on and on and on with no end and no significant change in sight? This thought-stream is known as *depressive rumination*. It is not a healthy path to pursue.

On the other hand, imagine that you simply take *this* moment, the one you are in, and hold it in awareness as it is, including any discomfort you are experiencing. Can you see that now the story is no longer the small, limited, inflexible story of you? That story may still be here, and it may still be true to a degree. But now you have a much bigger story, with a much broader perspective, admitting of many more possibilities. Can you see that if you can accept how things are now, the very next moment is already different? Can you see that it is instantly liberated from all the narratives we constantly saddle ourselves with that aren't the full story? The practice can bring us back to how it is in the body right now. It is experience based, somatically based, present-moment based. It is generous, wise, and open to possibilities, to not-knowing.

Acceptance, as we are defining it, is an expression of lived wisdom. Not that it is easy to accept what is unfolding, especially if it is highly unpleasant. But you can see that the shift to awarenessing with acceptance immediately frees us from the narrative in our heads that says: "I've got to have conditions be just so in order for the moment to be a happy moment." Such an orientation persists in clinging to ideas, opinions, and thoughts. But clinging is the opposite of acceptance. When we let go of having things have to manifest exactly the way we think we need them to in order to be happy or in order for us to even show up with awareness in the present moment — when we can hold whatever is unfolding, pleasant, unpleasant, or neutral, in awareness and allow things to be exactly as they already are, however they are — then all of a sudden it becomes possible for us to stand fully in this moment without it having to be any different. As we have seen, this rotation in consciousness itself is freedom, is already a moment of liberation. It comes from acceptance, but it is not mere acceptance. It is certainly not passive resignation, nor is it turning yourself into a doormat and letting the world or life or other people trample all over you. It is apprehending the actuality of things so you know what is what — or know you don't know.

Then in the next moment, if it is appropriate to act, you act. But you will act out of mindfulness, out of heartfulness, out of some kind of emotional intelligence instead of being hijacked by whatever your feelings are about what you feel you cannot accept. Or you won't, or it won't be as mindful as you hoped it would be, and you will learn from that.

It can take a long time to come to acceptance around certain issues — usually the hardest ones, the most traumatic ones. Sometimes you may have to go into and experience denial for a time; sometimes you may have to experience anger or rage; sometimes you may have to meet and accept your grief. But ultimately the challenge is, "Can I accept things the way they are, moment by moment by moment?" "Can I accept things the way they are now?"

7. LETTING GO

The last foundational attitude of mindfulness practice is letting go. Letting go means letting be. It does not mean pushing things away or forcing ourselves to release what we are clinging to, what we are most strongly attached to. On the contrary, letting go is akin to non-attachment, and in particular, non-attachment to outcome, when we are no longer grasping for what we want, what we are already clinging to, or what we simply *have* to have. Letting go also means not clinging to what we most hate, what we have a huge aversion for. Aversion is just another form of attachment, a negative attachment. It has the energy of repulsion, but it is clinging just the same. When we purposefully cultivate an attitude of letting things be as they are, it signifies that you recognize that you are much bigger and more spacious than the voice that keeps saying "This cannot be happening," or "Things have to happen *this* way."

When you let things be as they are, you are aligning yourself with that domain of being that is awareness itself, pure awareness. In this way, you are affirming for that moment that you are no longer the product of your thoughts and their endemic fixation on the personal pronouns. As we have seen, even thinking and selfing can be held in awareness. They do not need to be either pursued or rejected, nor feared for that matter. They are just thoughts, events in the field of awareness. Still, awareness can hold them in such a way that they don't have to imprision us anymore. We do not have to be a victim of our endless and unquenchable desires. When we see this, we can let go of both our cravings and our fears, we can let things be as they are, we can drop into being — and being this knowing. We no longer have to push anything away.

We may gradually come to see that this option may be the only sensible, sane, and healthy approach to experience available to us. It is immediately liberating. The more we let go in this way, the deeper our well-being.

The attitude of letting go, of letting things be as they are, of non-attachment, does not imply a condition of reactive distancing or detachment, and is not to be confused with passivity, dissociative behaviors, or attempts to separate yourself even the tiniest bit from reality. It is not a pathological condition of withdrawal adopted to protect yourself. Nor is it nihilistic. It is exactly opposite: a supremely healthy condition of heart and mind. It means embracing the whole of reality in a new way. But like mindfulness, and all the other attitudinal foundations, it is not an ideal or a special state. It is a way of being that is developed through practice.

As with all the other foundational qualities, we get plenty of opportunities to practice.

PART V

PRACTICING

Getting Started with Formal Practice

As you move into the practice itself using the guided meditations on the accompanying CD, you will be cultivating mindfulness moment by moment by moment as you follow my voice and what I am suggesting you pay attention to.

• • •

You will find that I am reminding and encouraging you over and over again to attend as best you can non-judgmentally but with great discernment to the unfolding of different aspects of your experience in any given moment. Keep in mind that it is the awareness that is always what is most important! Also that it is the awareness that is the common denominator across the selection of meditations. It might help if you think of them as different doors into the same room, which is ultimately the room of your own heart.

The best way to work with these programs and to cultivate a robust mindfulness practice is to make time each day to practice formally at least one of the guided meditations. Do it as if your life depended on it. But you can only find out whether that is the case or not by practicing regularly over days, weeks, months, and hopefully years. Since practice is nothing less than showing up completely in your life in the only moment you ever have in which to live, it makes sense to remember that whatever you may be temporarily giving up to make the time to practice pales in comparison to the benefits of inhabiting your life as if it really matters. So the way to undertake the practice is as an experiment.

I suggest that you give yourself at least six months to practice every day, whether you like it or not, whether you feel like it or not. While six months may sound extreme, actually it is being offered as a way for you to reconnect with and nurture the genius elements of your own being, all too easily abandoned in the pull of the seeming urgency of personal commitments, responsibilities, and unexamined lifestyle habits. If this appeal makes sense to you, then do it for yourself and for your love of life rather than to "improve yourself" and be a better person. You can't be a "better" person because you are already perfect as you are, including all your "imperfections." You are already whole. Nevertheless, you can embody the fullness of your being far more than you might have thought possible: far beyond your thoughts and mind habits; beyond the limiting narratives, the acquisitive narratives, and the addictive narratives that may at times dominate the landscape of your life.

It is best if you can make a time and a place in your home to practice each day that is sacrosanct, a time that is just for you, just for being. The guided meditations are not that long by the clock, so it is helpful to give yourself over to the timeless quality of the present moment every time you practice. It is the quality of your motivation that sets the tone for your openness to experiencing whatever it is that arises, whether you are featuring the breath sensations in the body as the major object of attention, or the body as a whole, or sounds, or thoughts or emotions, or when you are practicing resting in pure awareness, a practice which, as you will shortly see, also goes by a lot of other names, including "objectless awareness," choiceless awareness, and the method of no method.

Whatever guided meditation practice you are working with, I suggest that you follow along with my instructions as best you can, keeping in mind that they are pointing at constantly changing elements of your own inner landscape. For this reason, it is important to attend as best you can moment by moment to what I am pointing to in order to have a direct, lived experience of the object of attention in that moment and of your attending, rather than just mindlessly following instructions from what might seem like a tour guide. This is not about sightseeing, but *seeing* the sights. It is about *hearing* the sounds that arrive at your ears and the silence underneath and in between all sounds. It is about *feeling* your body. It is about *being aware*.

Although it might seem that there is plenty "to do" on these guided meditation programs, none of it is about doing anything or getting somewhere else. It is all about being. It is about giving yourself over to the present moment and to your own experience, over and over again, day in and day out, moment by moment, and even year by year. After a while it becomes a way of being that you would no more give up than you would give up brushing your teeth every day or being present with your children. The discipline can even become effortless. But I would give it ample time to take root, perhaps a few decades . . . at least.

And, of course, once you get the hang of it, it is a good idea to sometimes practice on your own, without my guidance.

FOUR SIMPLE RECOMMENDATIONS FOR FORMAL PRACTICE

So here are a few pointers to get you started and suggestions for how to work with some of the common challenges to beginning a meditation practice:

1. Posture

The carriage of your body during formal practice is important. It helps if you adopt a posture that embodies wakefulness, even or especially if you feel sleepy. That probably means not practicing lying down, although lying down can be a wonderful way to cultivate mindfulness and wakefulness as we do in various body scans and lying-down meditations. (Listen to *Guided Mindfulness Meditation* audios by Jon Kabat-Zinn, Sounds True, 2005, and the *Series 2 and Series 3 Guided Mindfulness Meditations with Jon Kabat-Zinn*, www.mindfulnesscds.com). If you set your intention at the beginning of a period of practice to "fall awake" instead of "falling asleep," then it is fine to experiment with practicing lying down. Aside from the fact that you can also meditate formally when standing still or while walking, a posture that embodies wakefulness usually suggests sitting, and sitting in such a way that the back is straight but relaxed, with the shoulders and arms hanging off the rib cage, the head erect, and the chin slightly tucked. You can sit either on a straight-backed chair or on a cushion on the floor. As best you can, sit in a posture that naturally and easily embodies dignity and presence for you.

If you choose a chair, try to sit with your feet uncrossed and flat on the floor, and if possible (and it may not always be possible) with your back away from the back of the chair so your posture is self-supporting, with the spine self-elevating out of the pelvis.

If you choose a cushion on the floor, you will need padding for your knees. A zabuton (a cushioned mat) underneath a zafu (round meditation cushion) is one good solution. If you choose to sit on a zafu, choose one with a height that works for your body. The idea is to sit on the forward third of the cushion, with the pelvis tilted slightly down, allowing the natural lordotic curve in the lower back to move in both a forward and an upward direction. Your knees may or may not touch the floor (or rug or zabuton), depending on how flexible your hips are. For comfort, you may want to support your knees with extra cushioning if they do not rest easy on the surface below you.

You can do various things with your legs. They can be folded into what is called the Burmese posture, with one lower leg draped in front of the other. That is the easiest, and therefore the posture that is least likely to cause increasingly unpleasant sensations with longer sitting times. (For drawings of various sitting postures, see *Full Catastrophe Living*.)

You can also do various things with your hands. I generally keep mine folded in my lap, with the fingers of the left hand lying on top of the fingers of the right hand, and the thumbs either lying one (left) on top of the other (right) or with the thumb tips touching. The latter forms what is called the "cosmic mudra," in the shape of an oval above the fingers. There are also many other mudras that you can try out, like keeping your hands on your knees, facing either up or down.

Remember that it is not so much the position of the hands that is important, but your awareness of the feeling of the hands in any position. That way your hands, like your legs and your back, will begin illuminating for you the landscape of your own body and the various embodied sensory qualities associated with the myriad of ways the body can position itself, both in formal meditation and in daily life.

2. What to Do with Your Eyes

You can be aware with your eyes closed, and you can be aware with your eyes open. Therefore, you can meditate either with your eyes open or closed. Both have unique virtues, so you might want to experiment with both.

If you sit with your eyes open, it is good to let your gaze fall unfocused on the floor three or four feet out from you or on a wall if you are sitting facing a wall, as they do in some Zen traditions. Let the gaze be still and relaxed. It is not about staring at anything but simply an invitation to experience the chosen object of attention moment by moment, whatever it is, and resting in awareness with the eyes open.

3. Sleepiness

Obviously, if you are sleepy it is best to sit with your eyes open. But it is even better to find a time of day to practice when you are fairly awake. That is one good reason to practice early in the morning, after a good night's sleep. You can also splash cold water on your face before practicing if you feel sleepy — or even take an invigorating cold shower. Since being awake is important to you or you wouldn't have made it this far in the book and the practice, it makes sense to set up the conditions as best you can to be fully present.

Obviously, we have almost no control over some conditions, like how much ambient sound there may be in your location. But again, what is most important is the quality of your attention and awareness, not whether the conditions are optimal. Still, at the beginning, it is very helpful if you can minimize sleepiness and, to the degree possible, disturbances in your outer environment. There will be plenty of distractions to work with inwardly and outwardly, no matter how much you regulate the external environment.

4. Protecting This Time

It is best if the time you choose for formal practice is one in which you will not be interrupted. Shut off your cell phone, pager, computer, and the Internet. Close the door of your room and make sure that others know not to interrupt you during this time. This is another good reason for practicing early in the morning, before others have expectations of you, when you can make a time that is devoted strictly to being, a time for nurturing yourself through non-doing and the cultivation of mindfulness and heartfulness.

Mindfulness of Eating

● ● ●

GUIDED PRACTICE
Track 1
Eating Meditation

● ● ●

Given the obesity epidemic and the vast extent of unhealthy and disordered eating in our society, there is now a whole field in psychology that is concerned with cultivating greater mindfulness in eating and in all the behaviors associated with it, such as food choices, portion sizes, speed of eating, social conventions and pressures, snacking, and unconscious and unexamined thoughts and emotions related to food and eating.

But that is not the reason we begin with an eating meditation. We begin with eating mindfully because this little exercise has the potential to show us a great deal about what we don't let ourselves experience in our lives, way beyond eating.

In this guided "eating meditation," we let a raisin become the primary object of attention, and we experience the universe of the senses and of the body in relationship to this one object in unusual detail and much more slowly than we would normally eat anything. The raisin becomes the meditation teacher as well as the primary object of attention, potentially revealing aspects of your relationship to eating and to food that normally lie beneath the surface of awareness.

The challenge in this guided meditation — and the beauty of it — is simply to be with each moment as it is: for the seeing, for the smelling, for the holding of the raisin in your hand, for feeling it with your fingers, for the anticipation of eating it and how that manifests in the body and in the mouth, for when it is taken into the mouth and how it is "received," for the slow and deliberate chewing, for the tasting of it moment by moment and how it transforms with time, for the swallowing when the impulse to swallow arises and you respond to it, for all the thoughts and emotions that might arise at different points along the way, and for the extended aftermath of having swallowed it. All the while, the invitation is to be the knowing, to embody that which knows the experience as it is unfolding, and to rest in that awareness, moment by moment by moment.

Mindfulness of Breathing

• • •

GUIDED PRACTICE
Track 2
Mindfulness of Breathing

• • •

We can bring the same quality of attention that we brought to the raisin — the same moment-to-moment, non-judging, non-cerebral, direct tasting of our experience, whatever it is — to the feeling of the breath moving in and out of the body.

In this practice, we let everything but our breath move into the background, into the wings so to speak, as we feature the breath sensations center-stage in the field of awareness. We place our attention on our breath in the body, wherever the sensations are most vivid. That might be at the nostrils as you feel the air passing in and out of the body, or at your belly as you feel the gentle expanding of the abdominal wall on each in-breath and its receding on each out-breath, or wherever else the breath sensations are most readily experienced.

Feeling your breath is very different from thinking about your breathing, and it is *feeling* the breath that we are inviting into the fore. As best we can, we "ride" on the waves of the breath with our attention as it moves in and out of the body for the full duration of each breath in and the full duration of each breath out.

When we lose track of the breath, as we certainly will, we simply notice what is on our mind in the moment we realize that it is not the breath anymore. Then we gently and persistently reestablish our attending to the sensations of breathing wherever we have decided to focus on them in the body. We do this over and over again each time we discover that the mind is no longer on the breath. And we do it, as best we can, without judging ourselves harshly for the mind having wandered and without trying to be "perfect" in any way. We are not trying to become a "good meditator" or a "better meditator." We are not trying to become anything. We are simply becoming aware of what is unfolding from moment to moment as we bring our attention to this simple (but not so easy) task of feeling our breathing in the present moment — moment by moment and breath by breath.

Another way to put it is that we simply let the body breathe itself — remembering that it's not the breath that is most important here. What is of primary importance is the awareness and the quality of your experiencing of what is unfolding moment by moment. Of course the breath is important, but first and foremost it is awareness itself that is being cultivated here.

It is actually a huge and radical act of love and loving-kindness to spend some time each day in this way: resting in the domain of being, fully awake. And of course, you can tune into your breathing for brief moments throughout the day, and in that way, bring greater awareness to your life unfolding in whatever circumstances you find yourself.

With greater awareness, you may find you are making different choices about how to be in relationship with your experiences of daily living at work, in the family, by yourself, and with others.

Mindfulness of the Body as a Whole

• • •

GUIDED PRACTICE
Track 3
Mindfulness of the Body as a Whole

• • •

At this point in the practice, we expand the field of awareness around the breath until it includes a sense of the body as a whole, sitting and breathing.

Whether the sensations in various parts of the body are pleasant or unpleasant, comfortable or uncomfortable, or so neutral you hardly notice them at all, see if you can hold it all in awareness, moment by moment by moment, without doing anything and especially without trying to pursue anything or make anything go away. We're not trying to relax, we're not trying to get anywhere, and we are certainly not trying to obliterate thought. We're simply resting in awareness, with things exactly as they are.

When the mind gets lost, we simply see what is on our mind in that moment and gently move back into featuring center-stage in the field of awareness the sense of the body as a whole sitting here breathing. We do this over and over again because it is in the nature of the mind to wander off the primary object of attention. It does not mean that you are a "bad" meditator.

Remember that it is in the nature of the mind to wave, just as it is in the nature of the ocean to wave. Your challenge, as always, is to rest in the awarenessing.

Mindfulness of Sounds, Thoughts, and Emotions

• • •

• • •

Just as we can bring our attention to a raisin in our mouth or to the breath sensations in the body or to a sense of the body as a whole breathing, so we can bring our attention to what is coming to our ears — the whole domain of sounds and the spaces between them.

The challenge is to simply hear what is here to be heard. We are not going out and actually scanning for sounds or privileging some sounds over others because they are more pleasing; we're simply letting sounds arrive at our door, letting them come to us. We give ourselves over completely to the soundscape, attending to whatever is here to be heard: sounds and the spaces between them, and the silence inside and underneath all sound. Again, it is the awareness that is primary, not the sounds, or your thoughts about where they are coming from, or which ones you prefer, or your emotional reactions to certain sounds. So the challenge is to simply rest in awareness, hearing whatever there is to be heard, moment by moment by moment.

From here, the guided meditation shifts to attending to thoughts and emotions in exactly the same way as we were attending to sounds: as events in the field of awareness.

Thoughts can have any content or emotional valence whatsoever. They might be about the past, or about the future, or even about why you're not finding many thoughts just when you are supposed to be aware of them, which of course is itself a thought. The point is not to look for thoughts but to be more like a "thought mirror," simply allowing thoughts to register in awareness as they arise, as they linger, and as they dissolve — allowing awareness to hold it all, whatever thoughts and emotions arise, and as best you can without taking any of it personally, as if the thoughts were merely sounds, or weather patterns in the mind.

Of course, we can bring mindfulness to our thoughts and emotions throughout the day once we cultivate awareness of them through this more formal practice. It can be done anywhere, at any time, under any circumstances.

The practice of mindfulness of thoughts and emotions can be very challenging because it is so easy for us to be drawn into the *content* of our thoughts and emotions and be carried away in the thought-stream. But again, it is no more challenging than any other aspect of practice, if you remember not to take the content of your thoughts and internal narrative and dialogue personally and keep in mind that, as always, it is the awareness itself that is primary. We are not trying to change our thoughts, or substitute certain thoughts for other thoughts, or suppress them as if they "shouldn't be happening," or escape from them; instead, we are putting out the welcome mat out for all of them and simply being aware of thoughts as thoughts and emotions as emotions — regardless of their content or emotional charge.

The awareness of thoughts and emotions is the very same awareness as the awareness of sensations in the body and the awareness of sounds. In dwelling in awareness, there is a freedom right inside this moment, without having to have anything be different from how it already is. By virtue of being aware, our entire landscape of the heart and mind is transformed, without having to impose any framework on our experience. Instead, we grow naturally into self-understanding, which can very much influence how we are in relationship to our experience, inner and outer, whatever it may be. We are befriending the mind and the heart as they are and learning to inhabit an imperturbable silence that is never not here — a stillness that is native to our very nature as human beings.

Out of this intimacy and this cultivation, healing and transformation unfold naturally.

Mindfulness as Pure Awareness

• • •

GUIDED PRACTICE
Track 5
Mindfulness as Pure Awareness

• • •

In this last meditation, we practice taking up residence in awareness itself, without choosing any object or objects to focus on in particular.

This is the very same awareness that we have been bringing to various aspects of our experience in the other formal mindfulness practices. This practice is sometimes referred to as "objectless attention," "choiceless awareness," or "open presence." There is no agenda at all in terms of what we pay attention to. Of course, there's no agenda even when we're paying attention to objects; it's simply being the knowing through the various sense doors, of which there are more than five, as we saw earlier.

As we've also seen, awareness can hold anything. It is like space. It doesn't take up room by itself. So it can hold thoughts or feelings or sensations in the body, and these can be either painful or not painful, they can be anxiety producing or not. From the perspective of the awareness, it doesn't matter. It is very much like a mother holding her child. No matter what the child has done, what the child has experienced, or what the child fears, the mother still holds the child with unconditional love and acceptance. Even if the child is in pain, the mother holds the child with total kindness. This in itself is comforting and healing.

In a sense, this practice embodies the present moment and the infinite because the silence itself is infinite and the stillness enduring and imperturbable. Awareness doesn't have to do anything. It doesn't have to make anything happen. It just sees. It just knows. And in the seeing, as we have mentioned, in the knowing of any arisings through any of the senses, in the touching of any and all thoughts in awareness, these arisings in the mind — whether they are thoughts or emotions or sensations — self-liberate, dissolve on their own. They don't lead to anything else, they don't capture us and pull us away, *if* we don't feed them.

So we simply (although it is not so easy) and with compassion (also not always easy) hold whatever arises and recognize and know whatever arises in awareness as best we can. You don't need to do anything. There's no doing here. Just resting in choiceless awareness, in open presence, moment by moment by moment… and reestablishing awareness if you get lost and carried away, which of course is bound to happen, over and over and over again — nothing wrong with that. Indeed, there is beauty in the activity of the mind if we remember that it does not have to define us, that we do not have to be caught, that the contents of the mind and heart are not personal.

This practice of choiceless awareness, like all the others, is an occasion to let yourself be invited into the receptive, empty, spacious, knowing quality of awareness. It is an invitation to take up residency in awareness and dwell here in this timeless moment we call "now" that gives us another dimension of being in which to live, in which to be touched by the world, and through which to touch the world and others in their joy and in their pain, in which to come to our senses — all of them — and wake up to the actuality of who we are.

Epilogue

• • •

As we learn how to stabilize our paying attention and how to allow objects in the field of awareness to become more vivid—to see them with greater clarity, to drop beneath the surface of appearances—we are actually learning how to inhabit and how to rest in this capacity for awareness that is already ours. It can accompany us moment by moment by moment as we journey through our lives as they unfold through thick and thin. Each one of us can learn to rely on that awareness, on the power of mindfulness, to live our lives as if how we live them in the only moment we are ever alive really matters. And as I have been emphasizing from the beginning, and as you will find out more and more through continued practice, it does matter.

We are very much in the habit of thinking of ourselves in small, contracted ways — and of identifying with the content of our thoughts, emotions, and the narrative we build about ourselves — based on how much we like or dislike what is happening to us. This is our default mode. The power of mindfulness is the power to examine those self-identifications and their consequences and the power to examine the views and perspectives we adopt so reflexively and automatically and then proceed to think are us. The power of mindfulness lies in paying attention in a different, larger way to the actuality of life unfolding moment by moment by moment. It allows us to shift from mindlessness to mindfulness.

In the end, the healing and transformative power of mindfulness lies in paying attention to the miracle and beauty of our very being and in the expanded possibilities for being, knowing, and doing within a life that is lived and met and held in awareness and deep kindness in each unfolding moment.

So as you continue with the cultivation of mindfulness in your life, may you, as the Navajo blessing goes, "walk in beauty."

And may you realize that you already do.

Acknowledgments

I am deeply grateful to my wife, Myla, for her keen and incisive editorial suggestions and her always discerning eye and heart.

I am indebted to two friends and dharma brothers: Larry Rosenberg of the Cambridge Insight Meditation Center for the phrase "selfing," and Corrado Pensa of the Associazione per la Meditazione di Consapevolezza (A.Me.Co) in Rome, Italy, for the phrase "affectionate attention."

I am indebted to Alan Wallace for the view of the Buddha as a great scientist, and for the metaphor of the telescope and the need to stabilize and calibrate it before viewing.

I thank Tami Simon, founder and president of Sounds True, for the idea to develop a book out of the original program of CDs, and for her patience, good will, and deep friendship.

I would also like to express my gratitude to Haven Iverson of Sounds True for so skillfully shepherding the manuscript through all its various editorial phases, and to Laurel Kallenbach for her careful and thoughtful copyediting.

Recommended Reading

Of course, you can begin anywhere in an interembedded universe. Anything can lead to anything else, and it is good to trust your instincts and choices. Sometimes the right book just falls off the shelf. Other times, a title jumps out at you or someone puts the perfect book in your hands at just the right moment. Any such event might signal a good place to begin, or begin again.

What follows is a far-from-exhaustive list of some of the most well-crafted books available from teachers, past and present, and from clinicians and researchers who have left unique and diverse traces of their love and understanding for us to follow — if we care to.

I have suggested something of an order in the first few categories (but not among the books in a given category) to build your understanding of the breadth and depth of the practice of mindfulness, its roots and expressions in different Buddhist traditions and beyond, and also to deepen your motivation to practice and whet your imagination when it comes to your own agency in relationship to the potential for mindfulness to contribute to healing the world, in ways both little and big.

Beyond these recommendations, reading-wise you are on your own.

Of course, you always were anyway.

These are merely a few road maps.

GOOD PLACES TO START

Meditation in Action
Zen Mind, Beginner's Mind
Wherever You Go, There You Are

THEN

How to Train a Wild Elephant

Seeking the Heart of Wisdom

Lovingkindness

A Heart as Wide as the World

Everyday Zen

Mindfulness in Plain English

The Three Pillars of Zen

Cutting Through Spiritual Materialism

Breath by Breath

Untrain Your Parrot

Arriving at Your Own Door

Letting Everything Become Your Teacher

Why Meditate?

Happiness

Real Happiness

A Lamp in the Darkness

Sailing Home

The Joy of Living

THEN

Joyful Wisdom

Present Fresh Wakefulness

Rainbow Painting

Hoofprints of the Ox

The Heart of Buddhist Meditation

Small Boat, Great Mountain

The Mind and the Way

IF YOU ARE INTERESTED IN MBSR
AND ITS APPLICATIONS IN THE WORLD

Full Catastrophe Living

Coming to Our Senses

Heal Thy Self

Here for Now

A Mindfulness-Based Stress Reduction Workbook

Mindfulness-Based Cancer Recovery

Teaching Mindfulness

Mindfulness

IF YOU ARE INTERESTED IN MINDFULNESS-BASED
COGNITIVE THERAPY AND ITS APPLICATIONS

Mindfulness-Based Cognitive Therapy for Depression

The Mindful Way Through Depression

The Mindful Way Through Anxiety

Mindfulness-Based Cognitive Therapy for Cancer

Mindfulness-Based Cognitive Therapy for Anxious Children

Mindfulness

IF YOU ARE INTERESTED IN MINDFULNESS IN POLITICS
AND ITS APPLICATIONS IN PUBLIC LIFE

The Mindfulness Revolution

A Mindful Nation

OTHER APPLICATIONS OF MINDFULNESS

Mindful Eating

Eat, Drink, and Be Mindful

Mindful Birthing

The Mindful Child
Living in the Light of Dying
The Mindful Path to Self-Compassion
The Stress Reduction Workbook for Teens

IF YOU ARE INTERESTED IN THE SCIENCE OF MINDFULNESS

The Clinical Handbook of Mindfulness
The Art and Science of Mindfulness
The Mind's Own Physician
The Emotional Life of Your Brain
Fully Present
Healing Emotions
Destructive Emotions
Visions of Compassion
The Mindful Brain
Buddha's Brain
Full Catastrophe Living, 2nd edition

• • •

Susan Alpers, *Eat, Drink, and Be Mindful,* New Harbinger: Oakland, CA, 2008.

Ajahn Amero, *Small Boat, Great Mountain,* Abhayagiri Monastic Foundation: Redwood Valley, CA, 2003.

Nancy Bardacke, *Mindful Birthing,* HarperCollins: New York, 2012.

Trish Bartley, *Mindfulness-Based Cognitive Therapy for Cancer,* Wiley-Blackwell: Oxford, UK, 2012.

Jan Chozen Bays, *Mindful Eating,* Shambhala: Boston, 2009.

Jan Chozen Bays, *How to Train a Wild Elephant,* Shambhala: Boston, 2011.

Joko Beck, *Nothing Special,* HarperCollins: New York, 1995.

Gina Biegel, *The Stress Reduction Workbook for Teens,* New Harbinger: Oakland, CA, 2009.

Bhikkhu Bodhi, *The Noble Eightfold Path,* BPS Pariyatti Editions: Onalaska, WA, 2000.

Barry Boyce, Ed., *The Mindfulness Revolution,* Shambhala: Boston, 2011.

Linda Carlson and Michael Specca, *Mindfulness-Based Cancer Recovery,* New Harbinger: Oakland, CA, 2011.

Chokyi Nyima Rinpoche, *Present Fresh Wakefulness,* Rangjung Yeshe Books: Boudhanath, Nepal, 2004.

Richard J. Davidson and Sharon Begley, *The Emotional Life of Your Brain,* Hudson St. Press: New York, 2012.

Richard Davidson and Anne Harrington, *Visions of Compassion,* Oxford University Press: New York, 2002.

Fabrizio Didonna, ed., *Clinical Handbook of Mindfulness,* Springer: New York, 2008.

Norman Fischer, *Sailing Home,* Free Press: New York, 2008.

Christopher Germer, *The Mindful Path to Self-Compassion,* Guilford: New York, 2009.

Joseph Goldstein and Jack Kornfield, *Seeking the Heart of Wisdom,* Shambhala: Boston, 1987.

Daniel Goleman, *Healing Emotions,* Shambhala: Boston, 1997.

Daniel Goleman, *Destructive Emotions,* Bantam: New York, 2003.

Elizabeth Hamilton, *Untrain Your Parrot,* Shambhala: Boston, 2007.

Thich Nhat Hanh, *The Miracle of Mindfulness,* Beacon Press: Boston, 1976.

Rick Hanson and Richard Mendius, *Buddha's Brain,* New Harbinger: Oakland, CA, 2009.

Bante Henepola Gunaratana, *Mindfulness in Plain English,* Wisdom: Sommerville, MA, 2002.

Jon Kabat-Zinn and Richard J. Davidson, *The Mind's Own Physician,* New Harbinger: Oakland, CA, 2012.

Jon Kabat-Zinn, *Full Catastrophe Living,* Random House: New York, 1990; 2nd edition, 2013.

Jon Kabat-Zinn, *Wherever You Go, There You Are,* Hyperion: New York, 1994.

Myla Kabat-Zinn and Jon Kabat-Zinn, *Everyday Blessings,* Hyperion: New York, 1997.

Jon Kabat-Zinn, *Coming to Our Senses,* Hyperion: New York, 2005.

Jon Kabat-Zinn, *Arriving at Your Own Door,* Hyperion: New York, 2007.

Jon Kabat-Zinn, *Letting Everything Become Your Teacher,* Random House: New York, 2009.

Susan Kaiser-Greenland, *The Mindful Child,* Free Press: New York, 2010.

Philip Kapleau, *The Three Pillars of Zen,* Beacon: Boston, 1965.

Stephanie Kaza, *Mindfully Green,* Shambhala: Boston, 2008.

Jack Kornfield, *A Lamp in the Darkness,* Sounds True: Boulder, CO, 2011.

Jiddu Krishnamurti, *This Light in Oneself,* Shambhala: Boston, 1999.

Donald McCowan, Diane Reibel, and Marc S. Micozzi, *Teaching Mindfulness,* Springer: New York, 2010.

Mingyur Rinpoche, *The Joy of Living,* Three Rivers Press: New York, 2007.

Mingyur Rinpoche, *Joyful Wisdom,* Harmony Books: New York, 2010.

Stephen Mitchell, *The Second Book of the Tao,* Penguin: New York, 2009.

Susan Orsillo and Lizbeth Roemer, *The Mindful Way Through Anxiety,* Guilford: New York, 2011.

Toni Packer, *The Silent Question,* Shambhala: Boston, 2007.

Matthieu Ricard, *Happiness,* Little Brown: New York, 2007.

Matthieu Ricard, *The Monk and the Philosopher,* Shocken: New York, 1998.

Matthieu Ricard, *Why Meditate?* Hay House: New York, 2010.

Elana Rosenbaum, *Here for Now,* Satya House: Harwick, MA, 2005.

Larry Rosenberg, *Breath by Breath,* Shambhala: Boston, 1998.

Larry Rosenberg, *Living in the Light of Dying,* Shambhala: Boston, 2000.

Tim Ryan, *A Mindful Nation,* Hay House: New York, 2012.

Sharon Salzberg, *Lovingkindness,* Shambhala: Boston, 1995.

Sharon Salzberg, *A Heart as Wide as the World,* Shambhala: Boston, 1997.

Sharon Salzberg, *Real Happiness,* Workman: New York, 2011.

Saki Santorelli, *Heal Thy Self,* Bell Tower: New York, 1999.

Zindel Segal, John Teasdale, and Mark Williams, *Mindfulness-Based Cognitive Therapy for Depression,* Guilford: New York, 2002.

Randye Semple and Jennifer Lee, *Mindfulness-Based Cognitive Therapy for Anxious Children,* New Harbinger: Oakland, CA, 2011.

Shauna Shapiro and Linda Carlson, *The Art and Science of Mindfulness,* American Psychological Association: Washington DC, 2009.

Shen-Yen, *Hoofprints of the Ox,* Oxford University Press: New York, 2001.

Daniel J. Siegal, *The Mindful Brain,* Norton: New York, 2007.

Daniel J. Siegal, *The Mindful Therapist,* Norton: New York, 2010.

Susan Smalley and Diana Winston, *Fully Present,* Da Capo: Philadelphia, 2010.

Ajahn Sumedo, *The Mind and the Way,* Wisdom: Boston, 1995.

Shunru Suzuki, *Zen Mind, Beginner's Mind,* Weatherhill: New York, 1970.

Bob Stahl and Elisha Goldstein, *A Mindfulness-Based Stress Reduction Workbook,* New Harbinger: Oakland, CA, 2010.

Nyanoponika Thera, *The Heart of Buddhist Meditation,* Samual Weiser: New York, 1962.

Eckhart Tolle, *The Power of Now,* New World Library: Novato, CA, 1999.

Chogyam Trungpa, *Meditation in Action,* Shambhala: Boston, 1970.

Chogyam Trungpa, *Cutting Through Spiritual Materialism,* Shambhala: Boston, 1973.

Tulku Urgyen, *Rainbow Painting,* Rangjung Yeshe: Boudhanath, Nepal, 1995.

Mark Williams, John Teasdale, Zindel Segal, and Jon Kabat-Zinn, *The Mindful Way Through Depression,* Guilford: New York, 2007.

Mark Williams and Danny Penman, *Mindfulness,* Little Brown: London UK, 2011.

About the Author

Jon Kabat-Zinn, PhD, Professor of Medicine Emeritus at the University of Massachusetts Medical School, is the founder of the Center for Mindfulness in Medicine, Health Care, and Society and of its world-renowned Mindfulness-Based Stress Reduction (MBSR) Clinic. He is the author of numerous bestselling books that have been translated into more than forty languages.

He received his doctoral degree in molecular biology from MIT in the laboratory of Nobel Laureate Salvador Luria, MD. Dr. Kabat-Zinn's research career focused on mind/body interactions for healing and on the clinical applications of mindfulness training for people with chronic pain and stress-related disorders, including the effects of MBSR on the brain and how it processes emotions, particularly under stress, and on the immune system (in collaboration with Richard J. Davidson, PhD, and colleagues at the University of Wisconsin). Dr. Kabat-Zinn's work has contributed to a growing movement of mindfulness into mainstream institutions such as hospitals, schools, corporations, prisons, and professional sports organizations. Medical centers around the world now offer clinical programs based on training in mindfulness and MBSR.

Dr. Kabat-Zinn has received numerous awards over the span of his career, the most recent of which are the Distinguished Friend Award (2005) from the Association for Behavioral and Cognitive Therapies; an Inaugural Pioneer in Integrative Medicine Award (2007) from the Bravewell Philanthropic Collaborative for Integrative Medicine; and the Mind and Brain Prize (2008) from the Center for Cognitive Science, University of Torino, Italy.

He is the founding convener of the Consortium of Academic Health Centers for Integrative Medicine and a former board member of the Mind and Life Institute. Most recently he published (with Richard J. Davidson) *The Mind's Own Physician: A Scientific Dialogue with the Dalai Lama on the Healing Power of Meditation,* and (with Mark Williams, PhD, of Oxford University) a special issue of the journal, *Contemporary Buddhism* (volume 12, issue 1, 2011), devoted to the subject of mindfulness from different classical and clinical perspectives. That issue was then published as a book, *Mindfulness: Diverse Perspectives on its Meaning, Origins, and Applications* (Routledge, UK, NY, 2013). He and his wife, Myla Kabat-Zinn, support initiatives to promote mindful parenting and to further mindfulness in K–12 education.

About Sounds True

Sounds True is a multimedia publisher whose mission is to inspire and support personal transformation and spiritual awakening. Founded in 1985 and located in Boulder, Colorado, we work with many of the leading spiritual teachers, thinkers, healers, and visionary artists of our time. We strive with every title to preserve the essential "living wisdom" of the author or artist. It is our goal to create products that not only provide information to a reader or listener, but that also embody the quality of a wisdom transmission.

For those seeking genuine transformation, Sounds True is your trusted partner. At SoundsTrue.com you will find a wealth of free resources to support your journey, including exclusive weekly audio interviews, free downloads, interactive learning tools, and other special savings on all our titles.

To learn more, please visit SoundsTrue.com/freegifts or call us toll-free at 800.333.9185.